Sicily as Metaphor

Leonardo Sciascia

Sicily as Metaphor

Conversations Presented by Marcelle Padovani

Translated by James Marcus

The Marlboro Press

First English language edition.

Translation copyright 1994 by James Marcus.
All rights reserved.
No part of this book may be reproduced in any form
without permission in writing from the publisher,
except by a reviewer who may quote brief passages
in a review to be published in a magazine or newspaper.

Originally published in French as
La Sicile comme métaphore
Copyright 1979 by Editions Stock

The publication of the present volume has been made
possible in part by a grant from
The National Endowment for the Arts,
as well as by the support of
the French Ministry of Culture.

Manufactured in the United States of America

Library of Congress Catalog Card Number 93-79805

Cloth: ISBN 0-910395-98-5
Paper: ISBN 0-910395-99-3

THE MARLBORO PRESS

MARLBORO, VERMONT

Publisher's Note

Marcelle Padovani, correspondent for *Le Nouvel Observateur* in Rome and author of *La Longue Marche. Le parti communiste italien*, recorded these conversations with Leonardo Sciascia in the latter half of the 1970's. Their first publication was in French, in 1979; within a few months' time there appeared, somewhat abbreviated, an Italian version of *Sicily as Metaphor*, published by Arnoldo Mondadori. Sciascia died ten years later, in 1989, at the age of sixty-eight.

Contents

Introduction by Marcelle Padovani	1
I. Who is Leonardo Sciascia?	11
II. The Mafia	35
III. How Can One Be Sicilian?	43
IV. The Writer's Truth	71
V. Concerning Power—Communist Power Especially	99

Introduction

The traveler disembarking in Palermo is immediately assaulted by an atmosphere of violence. The violence of certain graffiti on the walls. The violence of a sky that's too blue when it's blue and too scintillating when it's stormy. The violence, above all, of centuries of sunlight and an eternity of dust. The violence of the scirocco, the red wind blowing from Africa, which squeezes your head in a fiery vise while it covers the roofs, streets, and automobiles with sand. A wind so powerful that it isolates Sicily for an average of thirty days each year: airplanes can't land, the Straits of Messina are churned by enormous waves, the percentage of crimes of passion skyrockets, and people shut themselves in their houses. "Once there was a special room in old Sicilian houses," Sciascia tells us, "that was called 'the scirocco room.' It had no windows, or any other communication with the outside other than a narrow door opening onto an inside corridor, and this is where the family would take refuge against the wind." He adds this melancholy note: "The scirocco, too, is a dimension of Sicily."

In Sicily you feel yourself at the outer limits of the world. As soon as you cross the Straits of Messina the train begins to tremble on tracks that have suddenly become too narrow or too frail. The train's speed diminishes. The villages of small houses—Arabic, cubical, flat-roofed—clash with the mastodons that the building boom has deposited on every meter of land along the seaside. Here is the Arab face of Sicily with its Arab markets, its baroque churches and Spanish palaces—especially in Palermo, the magniloquent and tragic capital of the ancient Kingdom of the Two Sicilies. Here is Sicily where *camminare latino* means "to live an upright life." Where the Mafia performs the work even of the police. Where all the "feudal" repressions still could not prevent the explosion of *fasci siciliani,* the revolutionary socialist movement. And where famine-struck peasants stab themselves with pitchforks in order to attain the next world, while the aristocracy continues to squander its last bit of cash in Paris, a mythical (and, says Sciascia, "libertarian and aphrodisiac") city. Here, finally, is the "total world" that is Sicily: a self-governed island with its cultural autonomy, its peculiar economic resources, its own working class, customs, and writers: Tomasi di Lampedusa, Pirandello, Brancati, and, most recently, Leonardo Sciascia.

With Sciascia one seems to enter into a monastic atmosphere, in two senses. First, because his work is austere and devoid of formal concessions; and second, because it is swarming with churchmen: simple village curates or methodical embezzlers, dissolute priests or shameless impostors who don't hesitate to live in the lap of wealth and power, surrounded by damask, gilding, and polished silver. The vocation of this reserved and modest writer seems, oddly enough, to be that of provoking scandal—the same independent writer who chose a prophet's solitude as his vocation and first became known for *Le parrocchie di Regalpetra*, a kind of first-person testimony portraying the schoolmaster of a tiny Sicilian village in the years following the Second World War.

Leonardo Sciascia has always lived in Sicily. He travels to the mainland only to visit Paris, where he goes regularly (and this, too, is a venerable Sicilian tradition) to plunge himself into the political and avant-garde cultural life of the city that Sicilians have always regarded as the capital of Europe. He is animated by a consuming political and moral passion, and by a deep pessimism about the nature of power—but not about human nature. Seized, at times, by bitterness over the sluggishness of "radical" and "lay" political processes on the moral plane, he is anticlerical to the point of occasionally becoming Voltairean. ("Attentive to the fatality of names," he has written, "I can't avoid noting that the plague arrived in Trapani aboard a ship called *The Redemption*.") Indeed, Sciascia surprises us with the direct relationship he establishes between Racalmuto, that village of five thousand in western Sicily where he was born, and the world of the French Enlightenment, as symbolized by the Encyclopedists ("I have always dreamed," he confesses, "that I resemble Diderot").

All his work is saturated with the reality of Sicily, understood as a place of non-reason (and thus opposed to Paris, a mythical Paris unchanged since the seventeenth century); as a laboratory in which all experiments, even the worst, are performed; as a theater of eternal misrule; and as a testing bench for power. On the one hand, Sciascia attempts to link Sicily with the entire world, to translate the reality of its "world apart," its centrality, and its universality. On the other hand, he offers the world the prospect of its own future "Sicilianization." Sciascia in fact declares: "Everywhere reality is tending to become Mafia-like. The 'palm-tree line' is moving north from Africa to Europe at the rate of 50 centimeters a year. Heaven help us bear the consequences!" Is this the final prophecy from the Cassandra of Racalmuto?

In examining Sciascia's heroes one by one, who can fail to recognize his own neighbor, legislator, priest, or administrator in Rogas the policeman, Vella the abbot, Di Sales the lawyer, or Captain Bellodi? In the face of so many political perversions (which, alas, prompt a desire to "cultivate one's own garden,") who doesn't feel, at least at times, like Candido? But if there is a message in Sciascia's work it certainly is not one of resignation: born of explosive fury and deep indignation, his books leap into the fray rather than abandon it. Basically, as Dominique Fernandez says, the only myth that Sciascia sets forth is "Energy in the service of reason."

This author, who until quite recently was always classified as being at least in the Marxist orbit, is beyond any classification. He is first and foremost a brilliant technician, a skillful professional, one of those rare contemporary writers who knows his craft inside and out: the craft or art of "making himself read." Who has ever been bored reading one of Sciascia's books? Who can truly disregard the lessons in style imparted by his concise, brief, incisive, cinematic sentences? Along these lines Sciascia himself might say, "Diderot is my master."

Especially in the last few years, this solitary, often visionary writer has been known solely for his polemic with the Italian Communist Party, which has a long history. A moralist, thirster after justice, and impassioned lover of the truth, Sciascia was bound eventually to run athwart the PCI—that great bearer of culture and promoter of a "democratic revolution" whose moral dimension is among its most important components. As an unrelenting accuser of Christian Democracy's misdeeds, Sciascia couldn't fail to become one of the human symbols of the moral and political "housecleaning" that the PCI proposed to undertake in Italy.

Thus in June 1975 did Sciascia participate in Palermo's municipal elections, running as an independent on the Communist Party slate. He was elected, but it wasn't long before he grew disillusioned with the sluggishness and apparent incomprehensibility of political life. He retired, preferring to go on denouncing rather than try to manage such an elusive reality. But what was he denouncing, after all? The eternal "transformism" of politics, the lack of change, the obsessive repetition of situations? Filing through his work are "civic revolutionary committees" that hasten to enlist barons and bishops, revolutionary parties whose goal is to prevent a revolution. ("We must be realistic, Signor Cusan," says the head of the revolutionary party in *Equal Danger*. "We can't run the risk of a revolution breaking out, not right now.") We also read about drawing rooms where the minister of the interior mingles with financiers of anarchist plots, where men of the Left bask in the luxuries of the bourgeois home, where everybody resembles everybody else, criminals and judges, policemen and politicians. Reading Sciascia one clearly understands how power can come to seem so arbitrary, scornful, iniquitous, and arrogant.

For Leonardo Sciascia, it was the Moro affair and the irruption of the Red Brigades onto the Italian political scene that acted as catalysts, making clear as day a situation that confirmed his apprehensions, his fears about power, and also made him realize that the PCI had ceased to be what he had once thought it was.

At this point a rapid summary of the facts will be useful. When Aldo Moro was kidnapped by the Red Brigades on March 16, 1978, an enormous debate began in the realms of public opinion and the press. The theme of this debate: the "raison d'Etat." Should the state sacrifice Moro and refuse to negotiate with the terrorists, thus refusing as well to confirm their status as an "internal enemy army"? Or should it try to save the victim by accepting the terrorists' demands, since Italy was never obliged to defend the "strong state" position? The official line that came to be followed was actually the one supported by the PCI. The animating principles went like this. One can't make distinctions among individuals who live under the same law, one must not establish a differentiation between the citizens in one category, for whom the state is willing to make concessions because it deems them important, and the citizens in a second category, whom the state will allow to be murdered because they are socially less interesting. By killing Moro's five bodyguards in cold blood, and by continuing to commit crimes during the very period in which they were negotiating, the Red Brigades showed that their desire to bargain represented nothing but a further attempt to discredit the state, forcing it to assume a contradictory and unjust attitude in the face of its citizenry. In the end, the problem didn't consist of choosing between a "Prussian" state and a "humanitarian" state, but between the conservation or the destruction of the very idea of law. Not to mention the danger a democracy ran by institutionalizing such dealings with terrorism.

These were the themes around which the intellectual controversies developed. Some intellectuals were in favor of negotiations, others were not. Some remained silent, and were reprimanded for doing so. The left-wing newspaper *Paese Sera* had already written in its pages: "In these terrible days we are now living through, the intellectuals accustomed to spitting out sentences about the secret moods of the public consciousness are silent. Why?"—faulting Sciascia. And this was the period in which *Lotta Continua*, a newspaper of the extreme Left, launched the slogan "Neither for the Red Brigades nor for the State," defending a median position. The writer Alberto Moravia responded by acknowledging his "sorrowful estrangement" from the drama the Italian state was living through.

It was Sciascia who claimed that the admonishments going around were in themselves "terroristic." "All my life," he said, "everything that I've thought and written clearly shows that I could never side with the Red Brigades. As for identifying myself with the state as it is (and it would be more accurate to say as it has been since the kidnapping of Aldo Moro), it follows that I must say no." In any case, Sciascia thought that a state which was "incapable of protecting the president of the largest Italian political party, and which recovered his dead body fifty-five days after his kidnapping" had no right to be inflexible, either in its dealings with Moro or in its dealings with any other citizen.

The writer Luigi Compagnone attacked Sciascia in turn, explaining that the ill-humor and irritation toward the state of the author of *Candido* were an integral part of his Southern soul: "History . . . has been harsh to us people of the South." But this "estrangement" thesis did not convince Sciascia. Then *L'Unità*, the PCI newspaper, chimed in: "When the idea that one must support neither the Red Brigades nor the State prevails in the soul of the worker and the average citizen, then the terrorists will have already achieved half a victory."

Later on *La Stampa*, organ of the northern industrial bourgeoisie, entered the debate with an article by Francesco Barone: "Feelings are what they are, and can be changed at one's pleasure. But it's a different thing when, having made these feelings public, one wishes to rationalize them by searching for justifying motives." The opinions multiplied: Jemolo, Romeo, Fortini, Dacia Maraini, etc. But all the exchanges regarding what the state should or should not do served, at least in part, as an attack on the Communist Party, since the PCI was the principal defender of the refusal to negotiate.

For Sciascia this episode was, without a shadow of a doubt, exemplary. Behind it, in the wings, he claimed to divine a country that knew no way of expressing its disquiet. The PCI and Sciascia had reached their understanding on the grounds of virtue and the "moralization" of public life. But now it was a matter of political choices, and Sciascia and the party drew apart, apparently disappointed with one another.

Sciascia passed from a complicit indictment of errors and faults committed by a party to which he had felt particularly close, and for whom he had voted, to something harsher and more aggressive, as if he had definitively lost all hope. The Communist Party rebuked him for his attitude during Aldo Moro's imprisonment, for his refusal to defend the state, meaning (as the party saw it) democracy itself. The critics hardly softened their tone when it came time to consider Sciascia's writings, his published work.

It should be recalled that some criticisms had preceded the polemics about the Moro case. Prior to then, Sciascia had been taken to task for his way of making generalizations, his habit of beginning with an anecdote he considered emblematic and dissecting it in a systematic way. He had been reproved for confusing rationalism with good sense or common sense, which exonerated him from the necessity of coming to terms with history. He had been reproved for his insistence that "the truth is simple." He had been reproved for his inability to liberate himself from the ancient Southern traditions of skepticism and contempt for politics, which he always fell back upon to demonstrate the impossibility of change and progress. He was reproved, in short, for encouraging the kind of public indifference that always finds a great many takers in Italy.

Are these reproofs justified, in toto or in part? It is true that Sciascia is passing through a moment of crisis regarding his faith in progress, a moment of particularly deep disappointment in the accomplishments of the workers' movement since the Second World War. Anyone who knows the man and the writer cannot be astonished by this uneasiness of his: he is at once tormented and rigorous, even if appearances suggest otherwise. But perhaps for an intellectual of the South—or for an intellectual in general—it has become extremely difficult to find any solid ground in this final period of the twentieth century. It has become even more difficult, in the face of our ideological and cultural crises, to master—that is, comprehend—the sometimes absurd course that great political and social events take.

But however despairing Sciascia's reflections may seem, they remain extraordinarily stimulating: we can be sure this man will never forget that he is a child of the Enlightenment. And, after all, isn't it perhaps just and useful that the workers' movement should face the criticisms of this great Sicilian writer, and that it should learn to respond not only with polemics, but by demonstrating its ability to change?

—Marcelle Padovani

I. Who Is Leonardo Sciascia?

I was born in Racalmuto, province of Agrigento, in 1921, a year before the March on Rome. At first I didn't inhale much in the way of fascism, and my disenchantment began before I even started attending school. Every time my aunt's maid saw a portrait of Mussolini in the newspaper (and that was every day), she told me that his real name was not Mussolini but Musso-di-porco, pig's snout (she Italianized the Sicilian *mussu*). She hated him. And since I spent most of the day with her, being carried around or simply watching her while she cleaned, I ended up hating him too. Then there was another aunt of mine who kept a picture of Matteotti inside her sewing basket along with her needles, scissors, and spools of thread—she was always sewing. And every now and then she showed me the picture and told me that "he" had ordered Matteotti's death. She never uttered the name Mussolini, but I knew exactly who "he" was from listening to Totina (that was the maid's name).

I remember the day the last elections were held: there were a great many people wearing black shirts in front of the polls. Even my father wore a black shirt when he went out to vote, but he cursed as he put it on. The polling station was across from our house, and those black-clad men milling around in front gave me a feeling of fear. Surrounded by all that black they took me to the railroad station to see Farinacci, then secretary of the Fascist Party. And what's remained indelible since that day is my memory of the nickname a bystander applied to Farinacci: "the honorable Tettoia." That was the only time I heard it. People explained to me that the nickname alluded to the roofing, or *tettoia*, one sees on railroad stations. Farinacci, it seemed, had succeeded in becoming a lawyer only after becoming a redoubtable fascist. Before that he had been a stationmaster.

But things changed when I began school. First of all, you had to join "Balilla," the party's youth cadre. You were enrolled in due course and issued a membership card that cost five lire (a day's pay for a laborer or sulfur miner). You also received a uniform consisting of a black shirt, a blue scarf to be knotted around your neck like a tie or fastened with a medallion bearing Mussolini's image, gray-green pants and knee socks, and a black, tasseled cap they called a fez. I detested that cap. I always preferred to go bareheaded, and on the dampest winter days I wore a gray hat, high-domed and with a broad brim. My sister saved my first Balilla membership card: in the photograph I'm wearing that gray hat instead of the fez. It seems to me that with that card I celebrated the first nonconformist act of my life.

My Balilla membership, which obliged me to march around the school courtyard every Saturday afternoon with a toy rifle in my hand, didn't arouse much enthusiasm in me. I already knew how to shoot with a real rifle: my father and my uncle were passionate hunters, and along with their friends they always let me fire a few rounds at some target. I was a good shot until a few years ago, when I gave it up: using a small air rifle, I could shoot the head off a match at thirty feet.

So nothing I was forced to do as a Balilla member interested me. I grew bored and exhausted; I constantly fell out of step and was scolded and rebuked by the squad leader. But at school I felt a grain of enthusiasm when the teacher talked about fascism and Mussolini. According to the teacher, the world envied us fascism, it envied us Mussolini. And we owed everything to Mussolini and fascism: before, there had been only confusion, violence, and misery. Before, the politicians had been clowns and Mafiosi. Cowards, too. Everyone, in short, agreed that fascism was a great success—at school, in church, at home. But why, then, was I obliged to dress up in a uniform and march around the school courtyard every Saturday afternoon with a fake rifle?

I could go on with this memory game. But among these various elements of my sentimental and intellectual education it's best to nail down one fundamental point: that I passed the first twenty years of my life in a doubly unjust society, in a doubly unfree, doubly irrational society. A non-society, in effect. First there was Sicily, the Sicily whose truest and most profound representation has been provided by Pirandello. And then there was fascism. I tried to cope with being Sicilian and with fascism by searching for the method and the means inside myself (and, outside myself, only in books). In solitude. And therefore, by definition, neurotically. What I mean is, I'm well aware that during those twenty years I ended up acquiring a kind of "reasoning neurosis," a rationality that skates along the edge of irrationality.

Yes, I believe in reason. In reason, in liberty, and in justice, which together add up to reason (but woe to those who separate them). I believe that a world of liberty and justice can be realized, however imperfectly. But the whole of Sicilian history is a history of defeats—defeats of reason, defeats of reasonable men. And my history, too, is a history of defeats. Or, more modestly, of disappointments. That's where skepticism comes in. Skepticism isn't an acceptance of defeat, but a margin of safety, of elasticity, by means of which defeat—already foreseen, already "logical"—fails to become definitive and final. Skepticism is healthy. It's the best antidote to fanaticism. It prevents us from accepting ideas, beliefs, and hopes with that certainty which ends up killing off other people's freedom, and our own. One of the finest things ever said, especially considering the time in which it was said, was Montaigne's appraisal of the Inquisition: "After all, it means giving great weight to one's own opinions if a man is roasted alive for their sake." That's the most integrally skeptical thing that's ever been uttered: Catholicism viewed as an opinion, any old opinion. But, for the health of reason, for the health of mankind, this kind of skepticism is worth more than any certainty. . . .

I see skepticism, then, as the safety valve of reason. And so is pessimism, with which many people charge me. What fault is it of the mirror, Gogol said, if your noses are crooked? How can I be accused of pessimism when reality is so terrible? For at least fifteen years they've repeated the charge: "He's a pessimist." Now the moment has come for me to ask whether Italian reality (to choose only one) hasn't deteriorated during the last fifteen years and, furthermore, along precisely those lines my pessimism foresaw and warned about. . . .

Obviously I'm not made of pure reason, I don't live purely rationally (generally speaking, nobody does). The irrational exerts its sway, its fascination over me. . . . But I think we'll have an opportunity to discuss this later in our dialogue. For now, let me just say one thing in regard to the so-called New Philosophers: it's not their irrationality that interests me, but precisely that dose of rationalism evident in their emergence at just the right moment, and also in their proposal that we begin to think again, that we move beyond Marxism—the Marxism that, by now, all the parties have pissed on. What's more, I see the New Philosophers inviting us to return to the great themes of philosophy, and especially to the theme of death. The thought of death, Savinio said, is thought itself:

so, by removing itself from the thought of death, the world has somehow renounced thinking. It has also renounced civilization in the broadest sense, because no civilization can exist without being founded upon the thought of death. I'll go further: no life can exist that way either. I couldn't bear it. . . .

At a certain point, I believe around 1930, I managed to free myself from that obligation: the husband of one of my mother's sisters had been named president of Racalmuto's Balilla. Protected by my aunt, I no longer went to the drills on Saturday; I no longer donned my uniform. In Sicily, the function of family, with all its vast ramifications, is this: to protect its members, to help them avoid the duties that society and the state impose upon everyone. It's the main root of the Mafia, I'm well aware of that. But for once I profited from it, too.

From the moment I no longer felt the burden of being a Ballila, fascism seemed not to exist. People seemed to live with it like they lived inside their own skin. And let me tell you a truth, for me a terrible truth: even today I believe that a good part of the Italian people (on the Right, Left, and in the Center) would live with fascism like they live inside their own skin. Granted, a less choreographed brand of fascism, with fewer rituals and speeches, but fascism nonetheless. A regime that didn't burden us with thinking, evaluating, choosing. . . . Let's take a look at the election results from these last thirty years of democracy. A kind of instinct, similar to what Goethe called the German "sheepfold instinct," has guided the Italians in their search for and invention of a regime. Take the "historic compromise," for which the majority voted in the recent elections, and try to see what it means in the minds of those who approved it: a regime in which, finally and lastingly, the two largest parties reached a unitary management of power precluding every alternative and depriving every opposition of authority; and thus leaving the voters tranquil at last, irresponsible at last, at last freed of the obligation to think, to evaluate, to choose....

But this is a digression. Let's get back to the fascism of my childhood and adolescence. As I said, I no longer felt it after a certain point, as though it didn't exist for me. I realized it did when they began talking about the death penalty, the necessity of reinstating it for crimes against the state, against the men who dominated the state. I believed that jail—where so many, including my neighbors, ended up during those years of struggle against the Mafia—was the most severe punishment you could inflict on a man (and in fact it was). The idea that you could inflict death as a punishment disturbed and terrified me; the idea that you could inflict it in this way, coldly, by filling out a form at a desk. Not even the fact that men could kill other men: the local newspaper never lacked for murder victims. No, what disturbed me, what was for me a real and true trauma, was death through judgment, through filling out a form. It seemed and still seems to me the greatest infamy that could be arrived at by a society, a state, that part of the human race that consented to it, accepted it, or resigned themselves to it.

Naturally, I'm trying to decipher my confused impressions of that period, which I then experienced merely as pain, bewilderment, obsession. The death penalty, the death sentence, the firing squad—these thoughts and images haunted me every night before an agitated sleep extinguished them. And nobody wanted to discuss them with me; everybody considered them just. Then came the news of Schirru's execution by firing squad, the Schirru who had intended to murder Mussolini....

I've had three periods of long and heavy insomnia in my life, and two of them were earmarked by historical events: the execution of Schirru and, much later, the nonaggression pact between Stalin's Russia and Hitler's Germany. The fact that the death penalty also existed in nonfascist countries didn't mean a thing to me then. It hadn't existed in Italy, and then Mussolini enacted it. This led me to take a closer look at fascism, to glimpse the ways in which it flew in the face of liberty and dignity. It was a slow, contradictory, inadvertent process.... Take the war in Ethiopia, for example. It provoked a sentiment quite contrary to all the ugliness and ridicule I was discovering in fascism. It stirred a certain enthusiasm in me, both for the military enterprise itself and for the fact that Italy was being condemned and economically "besieged" by other states that were no less imperialist, no less colonialist. I think the war activated a kind of class instinct, a sense that I was part of a poverty-stricken people whom the rich wanted to stifle.... But not long afterward, with the war in Spain, my aversion to fascism became sharp and absolute. Not on an ideological level (because I've never managed to accept any ideology entirely, to reduce everything to it), but on the emotional, moral, and intellectual level.... However, I've already described my feelings about and reactions to those years in *Parrocchie di Regalpetra* and *Antimonio*.

My reading had an enormous role in the growth of my aversion to fascism. From the first moment I learned to read, I believe that I read—between the ages of eight and fourteen—every single printed page I could get my hands on. There weren't very many: no more than three hundred books in all, including those owned by my relatives. But among these three hundred were ten books or so that were essential to me: *I promessi sposi* and *Les Misérables*, Courier's *Libelli* and Diderot's *Paradoxe sur le comédien*, the Memoirs of Casanova. On the other hand, Rousseau's *Emile* had a negative effect on me: I found it false, conceived entirely apart from life. Nor have I ever succeeded in reading Rousseau without irritation. I felt an uncontainable joy when I first read a letter dated August 30, 1755 addressed to Rousseau from Voltaire: "Monsieur, I have received your new book against the human race...." I think I know it by heart. And I found other reasons for this distaste in Peter Viereck's book *From the Romantics to Hitler*.... Continuing to digress, I can say that my reaction to romanticism might be called genetic, in a certain sense. Sicilian culture ignored or rejected romanticism until the moment it arrived from France under the pretense of *verismo*, realism.

Among my relatives' books there wasn't a single one by a Sicilian author. The first Sicilian book I read was by Pirandello: *The Late Mattia Pascal*. I searched for it desperately after I saw the film by Marcel L'Herbier, with Ivan Mosjoukine in the role of Mattia and Michel Simon—very young, very gaunt—in the role of Pomino. An unforgettable film. I'd like to see it again. Mosjoukine was unforgettable.... Last year I strolled into Roger-Viollet, in the rue de Seine, and bought every photo of Mosjoukine they had. This actor has definitively lent his face and figure to two characters very dear to me: Mattia Pascal and Casanova. I'd like to see his film of Casanova again, too.... Another digression: movies, especially silent movies, played an enormous part in my childhood and adolescence. When it comes to my style of narration, my way of telling a story, I think I'm more indebted to the movies than to literature. But now I no longer go to the movies except out of obligation, to see the films made from my books.

Let's get back to Pirandello. When I finally found *The Late Mattia Pascal* and read it, and then read one of his collections of stories, I experienced a revelation—the revelation that I lived in a Pirandellian world, that the Pirandellian drama of identity and relativity was my own everyday drama. It induced a kind of mania, a kind of madness in me. Who am I, what am I, how do other people see me, what are other people like, how can I talk to others if they know nothing about me and I know nothing about them and nothing about myself as well?—these questions thrust me into isolation and solitude. To emerge from such a condition—which wasn't bookish, abstract, and mental, but had to do with daily life, with a Pirandellism found in nature—I clutched at reason, at the hidden other side of things, using the rational methods I'd encountered in Diderot, Courier, Manzoni. . . .

But here I am vastly oversimplifying an extremely complex, lengthy, and obscure process. I'm pulling it together from fragments, and who knows how reliable they are. Like everything we possess, memory, too, is a deception. Along with my vision, which in recent years has shown me distant things clearly and nearby things in a blur, my memory has acquired a kind of presbyopia. I remember things I couldn't remember ten years ago, and I distinctly remember events that are more and more distant. But is it possible that all these years haven't altered and corroded the things buried in my memory? . . . Here's another distant thing that I'd forgotten and now remember: my discovery of writing, the sensual, physical pleasure of writing; my love for the actual instruments of writing—notebooks, pencils, pens, ink. Curiously enough, I even remember the taste of ink. Maybe on some occasion I drank a little.

My grandfather was named Leonardo, like me. He was an enormous blue-eyed Lombard along the lines of Vittorini and, unlike me, a northerner. I've located his calling cards, which read: Leonardo Sciascia-Alfieri. Alfieri is a northern name, which he got from his mother along with his blue eyes, while Sciascia is in fact an Arab surname, which until 1860 in the official records was written as Xaxa. According to Michele Amari, in Arabic the word means "head-veil." Once the Libyan consul at Palermo told me that, in his country, the idiom used to indicate an extremely close friendship is "two heads under a single *sciascia*"—that is, a single head-veil. A few years ago there was a governor of the city of Oran, in Algeria, who was named Sciascia. Also: during a trip to Algeria my daughter was introduced to the Italian ambassador in the capital, and the ambassador, who was familiar with my name but couldn't quite place it (was I from North Africa? Libya?), exclaimed: "So you're the daughter of Sciascia, the writer! But have his books been translated into Italian?" I swear this is a true story. So then, my surname is extremely widespread throughout the Arab world, in Sicily, and even in Apulia, a region to which Frederick II deported a great many Arab-Sicilians.

My grandfather died in 1928, the year of Nobile's expedition to the North Pole. The doctor, the priest, and the entire family were present at the moment of his death, while I, in an adjacent room, was meticulously cutting out the pieces for a model of Nobile's dirigible. My grandfather had been a *caruso*, one of those kids who was employed to lug the raw material around in Sicilian sulfur mines. He first entered the mines at the age of nine, upon the death of his own father, and he continued to work there until the end of his days. The mine was terrible: stifling, deadly, inhuman. And yet, despite his exhaustion, when my grandfather Leonardo returned to his village after work, he attended classes taught by the priest. He learned to read, write, and do sums; he became foreman at the mine and then rose to an administrative post. Until just a few years ago many still remembered him, recalling his terrible rages, his refusal to cut any deals with the Mafia despite their threats. When the epoch of elections began, he even had the courage to come out against the Mafia's party. He never got rich, a fact for which his daughters scolded him, admiring him even while they considered him an idiot—an idiot for being honest, pigheaded, and incorruptible. It certainly isn't the least of the monstrosities of the old matriarchy in Sicily that women valued a man according to his ability to make money; they were expert at prodding him into every last dirty trick, every last compromise. I'm proud of my grandfather. There was a time when I would often be told: "Are you Leonardo's grandson? Your grandfather was an honest person." Honesty, a great virtue stifled by many Sicilians. My father possessed it too, but in a lower key. For example, my father enrolled in the Fascist Party in order to find work (without a party card, it was almost inevitable that you'd remain unemployed). My grandfather would never have done that.

From all I've said, it's obvious that I'm not in the least a "maternal" man, to use Savinio's expression. Could this be a reaction to the fact of having spent my childhood and adolescence in the midst of so many women, with my aunts and "mothers"? In any case, I became a rather "paternal" man. A great many Sicilians are like me. During their adolescence they have a contentious, even hostile, relationship with their fathers; then they suddenly notice, as if seeing themselves in a mirror, that they resemble their fathers, that they are repeating their fathers' existence. Guttuso, who is also a paternal man, once said to me, "Every morning when I shave, I discover my father's face in the mirror." Like me, he's noticed that so many misfortunes, so many tragedies of the South, come to us from women, especially when they become mothers. The women of the Mezzogiorno have a terrible gift for trouble. How many crimes of honor have been provoked, instigated, or encouraged by women!—by mothers, by mothers-in-law. Once they become mothers, they're suddenly capable of the worst acts of wickedness in order to perpetuate the very oppressions they suffered during their own youth; there's a frightening social conformity at work. "Fine, fine," they seem to say, "you're my son's wife? Well, if you dared to marry him, you'll have to pay the piper." In

Southern society these women represent an element of violence, dishonesty, and abuse of power, even if something of this ancient power was eroded following the arrival of the Americans in 1943. That's why my character Candido loses his mother at the very moment the United States soldiers disembark at Palermo. If this event delivered a body blow to the matriarchy, it was by generalizing and spreading "consumerism"—materialism, a taste for the good life and for home ownership. From the moment the construction of new housing began in Sicily, sons (and daughters-in-law) abandoned the old tyrannical hearths of their mothers, thus undermining, at least in part, the power structure.

My childhood and adolescence were permeated by this power structure. I should point out that, back then, every aspect of social life was strictly regulated. After nursery school boys were separated from girls: when the bell sounded they left school first: we, a few minutes later. It was difficult to have any kind of relationship with a girl: we were never together outside, and at home I was surrounded by other females! In fact, in my day, teenage love affairs never occurred outside the framework of kinship, beyond the circle of second or third cousins.

You flirted solely by looking, sometimes without even saying a word, but by exchanging glances.... You trailed your beloved chastely down the street, you spied on her from beneath her window, and, above all, you sought out her eyes. These glances were the equivalent of a seal on a lover's pact. In the school courtyard you sometimes managed to get away with a small conversation, of the most banal kind, of course—about classwork, for example—but so charged with tension that it was equivalent to a long amorous exchange. In this way you were absolutely assured of being able to preserve your love within the sphere of purest illusion. And if you then persevered to the point of becoming engaged, you remained under the ferocious surveillance of your relatives even during the engagement, never overstepping the boundary of glances. The possibility of a sexual relationship was more than exceptional: practically speaking, all of a boy's sexual baggage came from a commercial source. In our adolescent conversations about sex, the most bizarre romanticism mingled with the crudest terminology: in our arrogance, we were typical characters out of Brancati.

I remember a little blonde girl whom I loved very much, with a timidity equaled only by the violence of my passion, and who resembled a popular actress of the time, Simone Simon. This passion lasted through my entire adolescence, but I've never seen her again, not for almost forty years, although she lived just a few kilometers from Racalmuto. What's more, I wouldn't want to see her again; at this point the contact with reality would be terrible. Yet the memory is still a lovely one. Brancati says that "the yearning for a woman is such that one cannot endure her actual presence." Even the most piercing sexuality contains this undercurrent of fear. But this has nothing to do with my feelings back then.

As a matter of fact, my childhood closely resembles the one recounted one hundred fifty years ago by Stendhal in *The Life of Henri Brulard*. The Racalmuto of my day wasn't too different from Grenoble during the late 1700s. In Racalmuto the summers were extremely hot and the winters extremely cold and foggy. On one side stretched a bare and desolate landscape, the realm of the sulfur mines; on the other side, vineyards, olive groves, almond trees—untidy and beautiful. Against the cold there was a single remedy: a copper brazier full of burning charcoal. Against the heat: snow from Cammarata. "Cammarata snow! Cammarata snow!" you heard people shouting as soon as the June heat grew stifling. Cammarata is a village in the mountains, very high up. The snow that was collected there arrived in Racalmuto in handcarts, packed between two layers of straw and salt. The salt and straw served to isolate and conserve the snow. At home, too, the snow was covered with straw to make it last longer.

We used the snow to cool wine and water, and to make *granite*: a handful of snow squirted with blackberry or red currant syrup, which the children were particularly greedy for. You held it in the hollow of your hand and then quickly gobbled it up before it could melt. The *granite* made from Cammarata snow were a pure delight. At home there were also special bottles with an inside compartment one packed with snow, which meant we could drink cold wine in the middle of summer. When the ice factory was built during the thirties, on the one hand, the children mourned the Cammarata snow. But, on the other hand, they had a great time visiting the factory, even more than they would have had at Fiat: the chain conveyor belt, the blocks of ice slithering over the rollers—a fascinating spectacle. And then, for a penny, you were given a little crushed ice with syrup.

I began going to school when I was around six, with the sons of peasants and sulfur miners, but since I was the son of a clerk I dressed differently: I wore shoes even in the summertime. My schoolmates went barefoot, and they were literally swamped in the clothing of their fathers or older brothers. And clothes were so important! The girls never went around in bare feet, but this was because, shut up in the house with their mothers, they had less opportunity than we did to wear down their shoes on the cobblestones, or in the course of games—often violent ones. One of the more restful games consisted of tossing coins against a wall, trying to make them fall within a circle traced in the dirt. Whoever succeeded pocketed the whole pile. There was never any shortage of these coins: back then an ice cream cost no more than two pennies. We also played *bocce*, although we used stones because the real bocce balls were reserved exclusively for adults. Or we swarmed through the outlying gardens with our slings and projectiles: all it took was an elastic band—a piece of an inner tube—and a few stones, and we were transformed into so many Robin Hoods.

The sea was twenty-five kilometers away, and I saw it for the first time when I was five years old, at Agrigento. I didn't like it, and I still don't like it today. Nor do Sicilians in general like it, even those who live near it; most Sicilian villages ostentatiously turn their backs on the sea. How could such an insular people love the sea, which is only good for carrying away emigrants and bringing ashore invaders? That's why I don't even know how to swim. Nevertheless, it was during this trip to Agrigento that I experienced the revelation of what would be the great passion of my life—that is, the train. My astonishment was such that I instantly wanted to become a railwayman. That idea passed, but since then I've almost never traveled except by train. My longest trip? From Milan to Stockholm, meaning thirty-six hours in transit. But usually I break my journeys up into several stages: I love the sensation of travel, feeling the time and space of the voyage.

Our childhood trips took us in the direction of the countryside, rather than toward the sands of Agrigento. As soon as summer came into view, our hair was shaved off, and this was the signal that those marvelous migrations of the heavy Sicilian summer toward the trees on the hillsides would soon begin. They shaved our hair for hygienic reasons: the resin that dripped from the pistachio trees coagulated on our heads in clots that not even liters of petroleum could loosen. With your head shaved, that wasn't a problem. Thus we sat down under the trees and stayed listening to the insects while the resin trickled down, drop by drop, because of the heat. My family gladly went to the hill at Noce, a tiny property of my grandfather's, where I've now built my house. There were about fifty boys in the district, and we had wonderful fun playing together.

But school was fun too. It never seemed like a chore to me; I went there willingly, especially because my ability to solve math problems and whip off themes at high speed earned me a certain prestige among my schoolmates. My own preference was for history, doubtless because the teacher recounted it to us in a romantic, novelistic fashion. In any case, our relations with the teacher were always very cordial, except for the occasions when he rapped our fingertips with a pointer. No, I'm actually distorting my memories, because we didn't hate him even on those occasions. We cried just a little, very little, because we knew that the blows fitted into the regular order of things; we were perfectly aware that our fathers had somehow delegated to the teachers one of their main prerogatives, the right to thrash us. On the other hand, these things were part of a precise hierarchy: for the first two years of school we were entrusted to a female teacher, sweet and kindhearted, in a prolongation of maternal tenderness. After that, the teachers were all men. And in this way the perpetuation of the division of labor between mothers and fathers was assured, even within the walls of the school.

So I liked history the most. We began the third year with the Risorgimento, the wars of independence, Mazzini, Garibaldi, the Bandiera brothers. Despite it all, my favorite hero remained Napoleon, whose life was recounted to us in a truly Stendhalian manner. The teacher lost no opportunity to remind us of Napoleon's Italian descent: sure, he was Corsican, the teacher told us, but after all, wasn't Corsica an Italian territory? For us Napoleon was the positive hero par excellence. It was even suggested to us that, "like Mussolini," he had emerged from the rabble and made it to the top by his strengths alone. Napoleon Bonaparte in the guise of a fascist hero! No character in Italian history managed to fascinate me like he did; there, all I discovered were negative heroes.

When our teacher tackled the First World War, we delighted ourselves by contrasting his meticulous exposition with the personal epics related to us by the peasants! They saw the war as a disaster for which the students bore sole responsibility, since they had demonstrated in favor of intervention. I'm afraid that an absolute and irreducible distrust remained on the part of Sicilian peasants—and, I think, Italian peasants—in their confrontations with those accursed saber-rattling students. And this distrust still extends to the extreme Left today: to all those hot-heads, those crazies who get us into fighting wars against our will.

When I met my wife in 1943, she had just been appointed a schoolteacher in Racalmuto. A native of the province of Catania, she had passed the teaching certificate exam and been assigned to my village as her first post. I was twenty-three, she was twenty-two, and we were married in the spring of 1944. What a dreadful time! In Sicily the war was over, but it continued in the rest of Italy. There were shortages of everything: matches, cloth, and above all, bread. Deaths from malnutrition were common. Our wedding was celebrated with the greatest simplicity. No cake, no wine. A dear friend, who was also my witness, prompted an explosion of enthusiasm by offering us a rabbit as a wedding present, an inestimable rabbit. My marriage was an important event in my life, not least for the serenity it has brought me. If I've been able to write and work, I owe it in great part to my wife.

When our two daughters were born, we were forced to move to Caltanissetta so they could attend high school, and then later to Palermo, because they were going to the university. These were painful decisions for me, for I prefer to live in my own village, where everybody knows everybody, where you can be yourself, surrounded as you are by people who know all the important things about you.

    I also believe that village life is an incomparably rich source of observations. I'm thinking of the *"circoli,"* the social clubs: those privileged seats for the observation of other people. Fascism had transformed the *circoli* into so-called after-work centers, open to all "civilian forces." As a student I made my request for admission and was immediately accepted. The Racalmuto *circolo* is very old. You played cards there, you argued, you read the newspapers, but above all you chatted. Everything was marked by the greatest urbanity: aside from a little squabbling during elections, those gentlemen did not permit themselves the least impoliteness. (As an exceptional episode, one recalled that during the epoch of Bourbon rule someone had dared to punch the eye out of a portrait of King Ferdinand with a stick.) Women (meaning sex) were the main topic of discussion, and were talked about with maximum crudity.

    These clubs are full of characters who stand somewhere between Pirandello and Brancati with their ability to organize the game of being and appearance and with their underlying search for identity. An extraordinary character, whom I called Don Ferdinando in *Le parrocchie di Regalpetra*, frequented the Racalmuto social club. He was a small-time landowner who lived on his meager income and spent most of his time in the clubhouse. As a young man he had been a guitarist, and in the company of a violinist and pianist he "went up north"— the great adventure of his life—as far as Lyon, remaining there for almost six months. Paris, France—these were great myths, not only in Racalmuto but in all of Sicily.

    This small landowner was an antifascist, and he was a member of the last democratically elected town council before the advent of fascism. In earlier times, neither the March on Rome nor the figure of Mussolini had been taken very seriously in the village. Then came the murder of Matteotti and the obvious consolidation of this new power, at which point the scramble to climb aboard started. There were three political factions in Racalmuto. One, composed mostly of municipal functionaries and employees, was led by the founder of the local *fascio*; the second was made up of former nationalists; and the third, which included Don Ferdinando, currently held power in the municipality. At a certain point these last two groups also wanted to cast their lots with fascism, but had to contend with opposing factions among themselves. What to do? One day Starace, who was already a leader in the Fascist Party, came to Agrigento to choose between the factions. The two antagonistic groups took the same train to go meet with him, but when it came time to change cars in Aragona Caldare, the members of the democratic municipal group were so engrossed in discussion that they forgot to make the change and continued on to Comitini Bassa. There they got off to retrace their steps, but it was too late: the nationalists had already arrived in Agrigento, where they immediately enrolled in the Fascist Party. That was how the municipal democrats, by virtue of a moment's distraction, became antifascist.

We all love the place where we were born and are inclined to praise it. But Racalmuto really is an extraordinary village. Aside from the social club and the theater, which used to be host to the most fashionable companies, I love the daily life of Racalmuto, which has a slightly crazy dimension. The people are very intelligent, and they're all like characters in search of an author. I very much admire my neighbor out in the country, a wise and uncorrupt peasant who emigrated for three months to Germany where with a certain perseverance he would have been able to accumulate a small (very small) nest egg. Yet he preferred to come home, saying, "I'm happy in Racalmuto, it's a privilege to be here; I live well, I want for nothing." And when his father died he chucked everything out, television set, kitchen appliances, then he set about making his own wine, his olive oil, doing his own cooking. "Does this mean," I said, "that you've decided to live all by yourself, without any sort of woman at all?" "Look," he said to me, "I'm fifty years old. Before, there was my father and I was my father's son and now that I'm finally father of myself, you want me to take a wife and destroy the equilibrium I've just reached?" This peasant possesses great wisdom; he is uninterested in acquiring riches, in seeking for profits; his interest lies in another direction. That's the sort of man Racalmuto produced.

Why hide it? If I elected to be a teacher, beyond the obvious economic reasons (my parents hadn't the means to support me while I was at university, and so I had to choose studies that would be short and remunerative), I did so because it pleased me, or I preferred, to remain in the village. But I had no particular vocation for teaching, given that I'm little inclined by temperament toward communication. Originally, when I had to choose between working as a teacher or as a clerk in the state granary, I opted for the latter—which reveals the precise limits of my calling. But in 1948, with the abolition of rationing, the granary office was closed, so I took the teacher's exam. This transition to the schoolroom was difficult; then I adapted to it, and the students got used to me.

In those days the classes were overcrowded and the schooldays exhausting, especially during summer afternoons, but the worst thing was that at least thirty out of forty pupils were tormented by hunger. The sons of peasants, workers and sulfur miners, they ate bread with salted anchovies at noon and pasta or soup in the evenings. Talking to hungry children about such personages as Mazzini and Garibaldi, or lecturing to them on the Renaissance, was truly painful. For them school represented an indisputable constraint. But little by little they learned to trust their teacher and ended up telling me everything, even the most secret items—I mean whom their parents, brothers, and cousins had voted for. In that era it was easy, perhaps, to avow that one voted Christian Democrat, but it was more difficult to say, "I vote Communist." Yet the children understood very well that I didn't belong to the Christian Democrat camp.

After more than twenty years of teaching, I went to work in the office of a scholastic institution in Caltanissetta. Then, in 1969, I retired at age forty-eight. Since then I've devoted myself to the work of writing.

From twenty years of teaching what I retain above all is the memory of how difficult it was to arouse the children's interest. They were good enough at arithmetic, through pragmatic necessity (they performed little chores for the well-off, such as transporting water in fifteen- or twenty-liter galvanized buckets, or collecting eggs when there was to be a dinner party, and they systematically pocketed a few for themselves). Yet they proved slow and lazy in other areas, bestirring themselves only if you talked about everyday life. For them I chose poems in simple language, about soccer, about games, in dialect if possible, because these had the greatest impact on them. I knew very well that if they had any interest in geography it was because of its connections with emigration, and so I talked about foreign countries—Belgium, Canada. As much as the war, the calamity that destroyed the village (and continues to destroy it today) is emigration. I see my students again only during their vacations, because almost all of them are emigrants. In class we used to talk a great deal about the problems connected with emigration, since every child had a father, brother, or uncle abroad; and they were already anxious to join them, because, as they saw it, to emigrate was the natural thing to do.

Ever since the nineteenth century Sicily has been a land of emigration: initially to Tunisia, which is closest and where

Sicilians usually opened small shops. Frenchmen subsequently took over in that first migratory wave. The second wave headed toward the United States, and few of these emigrants returned. Then there was the hollow caused by fascism: from 1924 on it was forbidden to emigrate.

My father left in 1912 and returned in 1919, after having served in the ranks of the American army; in fact, every Italian living in the United States had been automatically called up from the moment Italy entered the war. I still have photos of my father in the uniform of an American soldier, with a broad-brimmed hat on. Before that, he worked in a huge laundry in New York, as, I think, a clothes presser. Yet at home he never talked about it; for him America was the unacceptable and the unspeakable. Once he had returned to Racalmuto he wanted to erase it all, as if that whole period had never existed. The few others who, like him, managed to return home, literally kept their mouths shut; you mentioned America in their presence and their lips would actually tighten. We never succeeded in getting a word out of them. The last thing my father received from New York was a check for a thousand dollars, sent to him by the veterans administration in 1941. He immediately left for Palermo, where he exchanged his dollars for lire—nineteen lire to the dollar, whereas after the war each dollar was worth nine hundred.

The people of Racalmuto have always viewed America with terror, as a particularly bitter and negative fate. Those emigrants who returned for a visit every five or ten years, and who seemed Americanized, were regarded with contempt, as if they had become stupider than before. America was imagined as a place where no one knew how to live, where you worked your fingers to the bone and brutalized yourself in the process, where your senses grew dull and you dressed in a bizarre manner: loud, garishly colored ties for the men, indescribable hats for the women. The returning emigrants could also be distinguished by their dated dialect; they called a jacket a *buinaca* instead of a *giacca*, or a fork a *burcetta* instead of a *forchetta*, and this evoked laughter in Racalmuto. And then they complained, saying the village hadn't changed, that it was just as filthy as before. And they looked down on us. They viewed their relatives with mistrust, as if everybody had his eye on their money; and perhaps that was so. In any case, all of this certainly didn't help the Americanized emigrants regain their proper place in the community.

This feeling in regard to America changed only with the last war, when the United States could cause us to live or die according to its whim. The children were dressed in American garments—undershirts, sweaters. We received packages of used clothing, or we bought them at the market or from traveling salesmen who came inland from the ports to sell us their junk. In those years my feelings toward America also changed, but in the opposite way. For me, the America of Dos Passos, Steinbeck, Caldwell, Faulkner, and Hemingway turned into the America that supported the worst men in Sicily, and the worst politics.

But today the emigration continues: to Canada—there are five thousand Racalmutesi in Hamilton—and to France, England, Belgium, and Germany. When their land of exile is in Europe, you can be almost certain of seeing the emigrants again; otherwise they're gone for good.

II. The Mafia

MARCELLE PADOVANI. You have written many times about the Mafia, and I don't want you to repeat things you've already said. Let me ask you: has your view of the Mafia changed in the last few years? How do you see the phenomenon today?

LEONARDO SCIASCIA. I'll answer by recounting three recent episodes that seem to me exemplary—exemplary also in the sense that they represent a point of view I didn't have before.

On March 19, 1961, Francesco Di Cristina died in Riesi, a town of about twenty thousand people in the province of Caltanissetta. His virtues and merits, which were known to the people of Riesi and perhaps the entire province, were unknown to the majority of Sicilians. And so they would have remained, had not piety and pride moved his relatives to have a *carte-souvenir* printed. This document immediately became famous and much sought after (one Mafialogist paid two hundred thousand lire for one.)

Certainly the relatives hadn't anticipated this. They had overlooked the fact that for some years the Mafia had been considered an evil, one that must be absolutely eradicated. Or perhaps they just didn't care. Besides, the *carte-souvenir* was supposed to have circulated only among friends. But when you have as many friends as Francesco Di Cristina had, there's always somebody who breaks down or betrays you. And thus the *carte-souvenir*, detached by cunning or commerce from the hands of the friend who is supposed to take good care of it, ends up in the dossier of the policeman and the sociologist—to no great profit, one must add, either to the policeman or to the sociologist.

It's worth describing this item and quoting its text. It takes the usual form of the funereal *carte-souvenir* and includes the usual emblems. On the inside, a photograph of Di Cristina, taken at least ten years before he died. An intelligent face; it must have been extremely mobile, moving easily from cordiality to harshness. Under the picture, the dates of his birth and death: July 18, 1896 and March 19, 1961. Opposite, there's an initial couplet in italics that says: "*In him men rediscovered / A spark of eternity stolen from the heavens.*" Then, in the shape and characters of a tombstone carving, comes the eulogy: "Realizing himself across the complete gamut of human possibilities, he showed the world how much a man could be. In him virtue and intelligence, wisdom and strength of soul, were happily joined for the good of the humble, for the defeat of the arrogant. He worked upon the earth, imposing on his fellow men respect for the eternal values of the human personality. The enemy of all injustice, he demonstrated in word and deed that his Mafia was not criminal, but respectful of the law of honor and the defender of every right. His greatness of soul was love."

From a purely external point of view, the eulogy possesses several novel and interesting elements (novel and interesting, that is, in light of the battle that a segment of Sicilian and Italian society has begun to wage against the Mafia). The word *Mafia* appears for the first time. And, what's more, it appears in a printed document accepted and used by the inner circle of the Mafia milieu, even if there's a distinction between "his Mafia" (meaning Di Cristina's) and other kinds, which, it is acknowledged, can be merely criminal. There's the assertion that the deceased realized himself "across the complete gamut of human possibilities"—whereof there is a great diversity, some of which are not always beneficial to others, even when illuminated and guided by virtue. (The use of the word *virtue* is neither casual nor improper. Mafia society is a disguised recapitulation of bourgeois society, and its virtues resemble those of the *Esprit des lois*.) Then there's the verb *impose* ("imposing on his fellow men"), which implies the use of force or violence, whether in pursuit of the good of the humble, respect for the human personality, or the defense of every right.

From this point of view, the document might appear naive to the point of self-destructiveness. After all, by now every single political party had joined the anti-Mafia coalition fostered by the Left—even those which maintained and will continue to maintain inextricable relationships with the Mafia. And scarcely a year later, the Italian parliament would create a special committee of inquiry to investigate the phenomenon of the Mafia in Sicily. So you might get the impression that the eulogy was the work of a hired scribe, one of those literary helpers to whom villagers turn when they need an obituary or a letter to a person of consequence. Furthermore, the scribe in this case seems to have been so out of touch as to prompt a suspicion that he was indulging a taste for double meanings and irony. In reality the document was an absolutely internal one, dictated by grief and addressed to people of (as Pitrè would say) "kindred feeling." The family didn't know, or didn't care to consider, how the document would be read and analyzed by those outside that circle of friendship, respect, and esteem that Di Cristina enjoyed not only in Riesi but also in the neighboring towns and in what Machiavelli would have called "high places."

That *carte-souvenir* was a mistake for the Di Cristina family. It attracted too much attention, and consequently forced those friends in "high places" to back out of a relationship that had become compromising. But it didn't make the slightest dent in the respect and esteem paid to the family by the citizens of Riesi.

The proof of this came on June 1, 1978, when about ten thousand people attended the funeral of Giuseppe Di Cristina, son of that Francesco who had robbed the heavens of an eternal spark. In the midst of a serious judicial proceeding, Giuseppe had just been released from prison on bail. Then he was mysteriously killed; so the police went to observe and photograph the obsequies, as did many journalists.

The journalists were greatly astonished by the extent of the town's mourning. "The schools and offices were empty, the shops lowered their shutters until the funeral was over, the movie theaters closed for two days, traffic was blocked for several hours, and the procession numbered ten thousand people..."—so ran the reports in the Sicilian newspapers. Among those ten thousand people, the pictures snapped by the police allowed them to identify forty-eight who had illegally absented themselves from work to attend the funeral. These forty-eight were denounced for their "interruption of public service." They included seventeen municipal employees, four district doctors, four school headmasters, five teachers, five postal clerks, two city employment officials, two tax-collection employees (one of the latter a provincial vice-secretary of the Republican Party), three officials from the National Highway Commission and one from the provincial administration, the town veterinarian, and four school custodians who had abandoned their duties to accompany Giuseppe Di Cristina to the town cemetery. In addition, the mayor (a Christian Democrat) and an official from the Department of Education (a provincial secretary of the Italian Socialist Party) were denounced for not having themselves denounced these absences. A municipal council clerk was also reprimanded for having permitted the town street-sweepers to clean the streets (and God knows how much they needed it) and to transport the innumerable wreaths adorning the ceremonies. And *dulcis in fundo*, two hundred students joined the sad procession. Had they spontaneously cut their classes or were they urged to cut them? It's a disquieting fact in any case, whether they were taking part out of grief or fear or simply in order to duck out of a few hours of school and enjoy the spectacle of the funeral.

Such an impressive display, such complete civic participation in the funeral of a man whom the newspapers had labeled a Mafioso, and who had been forced to respond to extremely grave charges, is worth more than all the printed pages—investigations, reprimands, articles—that have surrounded the Mafia phenomenon for almost a century. Every single citizen who took part in that funeral was well aware that he would now assume the role of a "friend" of the deceased, and that, with the aid of photographic records, he would remain thus fixed in the memory of the police. Yet these citizens didn't worry about the danger, in fact they challenged it. Why? Was it because the fear inspired by the Di Cristina family was much stronger than that inspired by the police, the state, the laws of the state?

There's no point in fooling ourselves: fear had practically nothing to do with it. The behavior of the population of Riesi can be explained in only one way. The *carabinieri*, the state, the law of the state, were somehow nonexistent in the face of that funeral, as if they had vanished. The uniformed *carabinieri* and the plainclothes police who were there to observe, to take photos of the participants, lacked any importance. For the citizens of Riesi that ceremony was expressive of their life, of their mode of being, of their vision of things; it was a function of the one law they truly knew—a moral and practical law, ruling affections and effects, in both the interior and the social order.

For comparison (and verification), here is an event that took place almost a year later in Palermo. Michele Reina, provincial secretary of the Christian Democrats and head of the city council, was killed this year on the evening of March 9. An hour later, in a telephone call to the *Giornale di Sicilia*, the left-wing Prima Linea group took credit for the killing: "We have executed the Mafioso Michele Reina." At first the telephone call was considered reliable. Within hours, though, doubts began to appear. These doubts were based on two convictions. First, in a city like Palermo, dominated by the Mafia, protected by the Mafia, a subversive group could not possibly conduct such an elaborate operation with impunity. In the south of Italy, of course, the police are incapable of preventing such actions or arresting the culprits. But it's unthinkable that the Mafia, which knows and sees everything, availing itself of a perfect capillary network of information, could be taken by surprise.

And second, the killing of a Christian Democrat must necessarily stem from internal motives—an intraparty feud involving personal power or professional turf. Perhaps it involved the candidacy for the imminent elections to the national and European parliaments, or bribes on public works contracts. In any case, the fact that Christian Democrats have been killed or kneecapped by subversive groups in other parts of Italy makes no difference. In Sicily it's something else, it's always something else.

Within a few days these doubts had become certainties. Everybody decided that Michele Reina hadn't been killed by Prima Linea; everybody decided that he'd been killed by the Mafia, or by a part of the Mafia caught in an internal conflict, or for Mafia-related reasons. The police seemed certain of this, too; and the Christian Democrats extremely certain. In this certainty the entire city heaved a sigh of relief.

There is no single precise detail upon which so much certainty can be founded. In fact there are two details, if rather vague ones, which suggest exactly the opposite conclusion. First, the hasty and makeshift character of the operation: it was conducted with a car stolen that very day, outfitted with license plates that were also stolen that day. Then there's the use of the word *Mafioso* in the telephone call to the newspaper, which a true Mafioso, supposing that he had made the call to confuse the investigation, would refuse to pronounce even in his dreams or under torture. (As we've seen, its unexpected use in Di Cristina's *carte-souvenir* was an exception, dictated by grief.) Yet we still feel an immediate need to reconstruct the illusion of an efficient, protective Mafia, unchanging and unchangeable. Only from the Left does there emerge an alternative hypothesis, formally different but substantially confirming the image of an omnipotent Mafia, without whose assent no criminal act is possible. According to this hypothesis, the Mafia and the terrorists are allied, or the Mafia has deliberately given the terrorists a free hand. A ridiculous theory, advanced with incredible seriousness.

Naturally we can't confirm beyond any doubt that Michele Reina was assassinated by Prima Linea rather than the Mafia (or by one Mafia *cosca* in conflict with others.) But the fact that an entire city rested easier in the certainty that he was killed by the Mafia—without a shred of evidence—is something to consider when trying to explain the stubborn persistence of the Mafia phenomenon.

III. How Can One Be Sicilian?

MARCELLE PADOVANI. "How can one be a Sicilian?" So exclaims the viceroy of Sicily when he leaves Palermo after the turbulent incident of the "San Martino codices." To this day one notes a similar astonishment among many foreigners and even Italians. What does it mean to be a Sicilian? What are the fundamental traits of the Sicilian's psychology that have persisted throughout the centuries? Is the whole of Italy on the verge of becoming Sicilian, in accordance with the "palm-tree line" that "is mounting from the south to the north at the rate of fifty meters a year"? What of the portrait of Sicily that can be gleaned from your books—are its elements still present? And above all, what about Sicily's apparently irremediable underdevelopment?

"Sicily is a bitter land," you write in *Le parrocchie di Regalpetra*. "Roads and houses have been built, and even Regalpetra is blessed with asphalt and new buildings, but in the end you can't say that the human situation has changed much since the days of Phillip II." Your work teems with evidence of such "modern misery." Furthermore, there is in your description of Sicily a dreamlike quality; at times you say that "all of Sicily is a fantastical dimension." And you add: "How can one live there without imagination?" On the other hand, your characters often devote themselves to denying the truth, to reconstructing it, for example, with imposture. Why does this secret Sicily need to dream, to flee the sphere of the real?

I must also emphasize your persistent attempt to clarify the passion for the "juridical" that animates your fellow citizens. "In Sicily," you write, "the crime of passion is not born from a true and proper passion, from the passion of the heart, but from a kind of intellectual passion—a preoccupation with, so to speak, juridical formalities." Thus we learn that the inhabitant of Regalpetra with half an hour to kill in the city will not forget to drop in at the courthouse, even at the risk of missing his train. Can such a passion for the juridical derive from the fact that Sicily, like other Mediterranean countries, is a "land of forums," where everything is resolved in the public piazza? Or does it express a desperate will to resist isolation, whence comes this excessive respect for "forums"?

In the portrait of the typical Sicilian, also exists, obviously, the decisive role of woman and the family. "*Cherchez la femme*," one generally hears in Sicily. Yet as you write in *The Day of the Owl*: "In Sicily, thought Captain Bellodi, it's not necessary to search for the woman, seeing that you always end up finding her, and in spite of the law." In your story "A Matter of Conscience," the search for the adulterous woman straightaway ends up involving a whole circle of gentlemen. How can we explain this Sicily of gossip, adultery, sexual taboos, and vendettas, where fathers, lovers, brothers, and husbands go so far as to forbid confession to their women? Why does woman seem to be an at once central and nonexistent figure in Sicilian mentality?

And why, in compensation, is the family affirmed as the only "truly living institution"? It's as if, in the Sicilian's natural solitude, he lacks any means other than the family to adapt himself to communal life. Perhaps it's a kind of behavior that by its very nature renders the Sicilian "schizophrenic," in the sense that it keeps him from establishing a connection between public and private life. In *The American Aunt*, for example, one of the characters declares: "I don't say a thing,

I keep my own counsel. Even if I see people walking around with their heads down, I don't open my mouth." In short, might not the cult of the family be the principal source of indifference to politics, of *qualunquismo*?

Finally, this gallery of Sicilian portraits and sentiments includes the idea of decadence. The aristocracy of the island has been a disappointment: it hasn't even been able to safeguard its privileges, has gambled away the last of its cash in the French casinos, and its palaces are falling into ruin. Yet the ruling class formed by functionaries of the central government is certainly no less disappointing. Has there been a period in her history when Sicily has not had to suffer an identity crisis? Has Sicily always been the symbol of "defeated" insularity, in contrast to the "victorious" insularity of England?

LEONARDO SCIASCIA. With a touch of malice, I made my character Candido lose his mother at the moment the Americans disembarked in Sicily, which therefore coincided with the beginning of the end of the redoubtable Sicilian matriarchy: it was then that woman lost her destructive power, a power that had become damaging also to her. Of all the developments it has been given me to witness, certainly one of the most significant is the end of this invisible power. Obviously it's not the only one, but the others have proven to be more accidental than substantial: they are changes that I would call passive, owing to the force of things or the course that events have chanced to take. Emigration, for example. On the other hand, I'm not underestimating the role of emigration in the desacralization of women. No longer having about grown sons or a husband to terrorize, finding herself alone on the land that had to be made to produce, with young children that had to be brought up, and dealings with a bureaucracy that needed to be conducted successfully—a series of tasks formerly reserved for the man—the Sicilian woman has acquired, thanks to emigration, a little more understanding, and consequently a little more freedom. Real freedom, I mean: not the dramatic and self-destructive kind that comes from ordering others around.

What's more, emigration has helped to raise the standard of living and to bring Sicily into the universe of consumerism. Those tiny sums sent every month by the emigrants have ensured that today the mean standard of living on the island does not differ substantially from that in the other regions of Italy. The paradoxical aspect of this phenomenon is that the one hundred fifty thousand or more who decided to leave Sicily to earn a living elsewhere lead exactly the same type of existence abroad that they would have led in Sicily thirty or forty years ago: an existence of privation, in which the material comforts are reduced to an absolute minimum, and the work is hard labor. They endure all this in order to set aside a measly nest egg, which inflation and the banks will whittle away before the emigrants can treat their families to its beneficent effects. These days, then, there are fifty or sixty thousand Sicilians who live worse than they did when they were in their own villages. But, by surviving on less and less, they allow their families to maintain a European standard of living. A kind of modern slavery: voluntary, necessary, and apparently impossible to eliminate.

If I use my own village as a yardstick, I can easily list the changes introduced by consumerism: the television and the appliances in every house, the automobiles parked out front. We are better able to take vacations, we live in more comfortable houses, we drink more, we eat more meat. When I was young, we butchered meat once a week, on Fridays—a cow, a few rams or goats. Today there's not a butcher who doesn't sell veal, slaughtering two or three times a week. The same thing happened with the caffès. Once the people who frequented them were considered idlers or spendthrifts, prone to throwing their money out the window. And there was only one caffè. Now there are five, and everybody goes to them. Not to mention the banks: once there was only one, the Bank of Sicily; but now there are two of them, and in certain villages you'll find no fewer than four or five. If you then keep in mind that the deposits in each of these banks amount to about twenty billion lire, you can figure out that the average savings per capita comes to ten million lire. Where does this money come from? From the emigrants, for a start. From the severance payments that the region—meaning the regional authorities who were so inclined—supposedly disbursed at the time the sulfur mines closed. From pensions. And also from the earnings of shopkeepers.

Yet despite it all, there are no rich people in Racalmuto. If the rate of savings is so high, part of the reason must be because the only thing we spend money on is the construction of new houses. (My neighbors have never heard a word of what are called equity loans, and the sole collective improvement that has been attempted concerns viticulture.) The Mafia, already decimated some time ago by the initiatives of Inspector Mori, can find no way to get their hands on this immovable cash: how can they extract their customary cut from sums earned outside of their own sphere, in Cologne or Paris?

So the change, in Racalmuto and in Sicily, has been made possible by isolation—by the marginalization of some hundred thousand individuals. What a strange thing! Men who procure the good life and who are at the root of the change, but who themselves have not changed; who experience the reality of foreign countries as if they were in vitro, and who conserve deep within themselves the psychology, mentality, and mechanisms of long ago.

In Sicily there has always been the aspiration toward at

least a more just world. Some have solved (or believed they have solved) the problem through emigration; others, through the mythic exaltation of far away realities. The latter solution explains the "Continent"—meaning mainland Italy. The Continent is an impossibly lofty place, evocative for Sicilians of a freer world, opposed to prejudice, injustice, and violence, where every person is cognizant of his rights and sees them respected. This dream also has its linguistic side: the idea of a single unifying language, capable of making everybody equal. If everyone spoke the same Italian, social and cultural differences would be abolished. It's the Italian language as a dream of justice.... Alas, in Sicily, only the employers, the bureaucrats, the officers, and the teachers speak Italian; and dialect belongs to the poorer classes, to serfs, workers, and peasants

Women have always been a part of this continental myth. It was imagined that continental women were necessarily freer, more accessible and less encumbered by prejudice. Off Sicilians went, then, in search of this supposed availability of continental women, but no way in the world would they accept that this turn into the availability of Sicilian women too. On the subject of women, on the perpetual desire for women, one must read Brancati. Brancati had married an Italian actress and, as a Sicilian, suffered horribly from this marriage, notwithstanding the level of consciousness and creativity he had attained. In Nino Martoglio's comedy *L'aria del continente* we again encounter this myth of the continental woman. It's the story of a rich Sicilian landowner who meets a woman up north, a woman so marvelous as to make him lose his head. He brings her back to Catania, marries her, commits a thousand follies for her. Immediately she becomes an object of envy on the part of his friends: they admire her, are jealous of her, and make her into the model of all that a desirable woman should be. At a certain point, however, it's suddenly revealed that this marvelous continental woman, this woman who expresses herself in Italian, who is thus fundamentally other than a Sicilian woman, was actually born in the municipality of Valguarnera Caropepe, in the province of Enna, just a few kilometers from Catania. Whereupon the myth crumbles, the love dies, the friends leave. "Carrapipana!" cries the landowner—"Woman of Caropepe!"—and, arms outflung, he confesses to his deep and indelible shame as the curtain comes down: he thought he had married a continental, and he finds himself hitched to an islander! Martoglio's comedy was an enormous success in Sicily. Indeed, he elaborated it from an idea he got from Pirandello, who let him have it for five hundred lire.

A goodly share of the dreams of Sicilian men continue to center around women. A certain type of behavior toward women persists like a categorical imperative: one is a true Sicilian if one *has* women, if one is obsessed with them, since this is the nature of a real man. Tormented by profound insecurity, by existential terror, by a fundamental instability, the Sicilian must perforce respond to the call of sex. Revolving around sexuality, however, is the religious (or, more accurately, pious) idea of the family, with woman as its organizing nucleus. Thus the woman is desired as a woman only insofar as she is *other* (or somebody else's, or nobody's, but never in any case her own self). Yet, once she becomes a wife, she is suddenly transfigured into an institution; she is transformed into family and vanishes as an individual woman.

This desire for women plays a role in the great Sicilian madness, to which Tomasi di Lampedusa is an outstanding witness. The Sicilian is intimately convinced that he is "the best" when it comes to matters of love and sexuality—convinced that he is sharper, shrewder, quicker, and more active than his competitors—and that Sicilians know how to love women and satisfy them better than anybody else. Certain of this superiority, he has a single desire: to show himself equal to his reputation for availability and quickness. The Sicilian's sexual behavior reveals something of a watermark of peasant civilization: the image of the "cock" that has developed in the realm of amorous relationships. In the peasant world the rooster represents the animal endowed with perfect sexuality—ready, speedy, insatiable, and capable of responding expertly to every request. It's obvious, then, why with the Sicilian the sexual act often reduces itself to not very much at all, in any case practiced without a great deal of pleasure, an act fleeting or even painful in its tragic brevity; and how sexuality, never being enjoyed as such, belongs to the world of the unreal. At the University of Heidelberg they conducted studies of couples made up of Sicilian men and German women. The researchers discovered that even in Heidelberg, the Sicilians continued to be convinced of their indomitable sexual superiority and their unbeatable rapidity, although the German women found no cause for contentment in performances so incomparably swift.

Another dimension of the dream, of the madness—and a further expression of a childish need for recognition and identity—is the exasperated "juridicalism" that unendingly plagues the island. When one reads in Cicero that "rhetoric had its origin in Sicily" and that Sicilians are a "people of sharp and suspicious genius, born for controversy," you have the feeling that he's talking about the Sicily of today, that the island has always been what it is, and that centuries of historic stratification have not changed it much nor for the better. One has much the same impression when one leafs through the *Treatise on the Character of the Sicilians* written in the sixteenth century by Scipio de Castro, who provides Marco Antonio Colonna, the newly appointed viceroy, with no end of warnings. Said Scipio: "The Sicilians as a whole are timid in the utilization of their personal wealth and prodigal in the use of public funds." Then there's the Tuscan Giovanni Maria Cecchi, also of the sixteenth century, who very well conveys this impression of a human reality that remains immobile in the face of invasions, wars, epidemics, disasters. The specific characteristics vary, of course, depending on whether one refers to the Arab domination, which brought about the prevalence of the fantastical and imaginative spirit, or Roman civilization, with its accent on collective organization and rules for life and behavior. When a Sicilian lives an upright life, it's described by the phrase *camminare latino*; leading an exceedingly upright life is *camminare latino latino*. On scales, the counterweight is still called the *romano*. All that in order to say how deeply the Sicilian soul was impressed by Roman law. However, if I had to sum up in a few words all that I have said, I would maintain that the Sicilians, despite the invasions, have been on the whole impermeable to foreign domination, and that an authentic Sicilian identity has managed to come down through the centuries.

You find it on the level of artistic expression, and it bears the name "realism," for art comes alive in Sicily with realism, with Antonello da Messina, then with the *verismo* of Giovanni Verga. This special attentiveness to the real—you find it even in the latter-day "Palermo school" of photography, with its fulgurations worthy of Cartier-Bresson, and in that great realistic painter Renato Guttuso. Movements, individual personalities, sometimes underrated, especially abroad—but the isolation they suffer from derives from the isolation in which Sicilian society maintains them: amongst us, the artist, the intellectual, the writer have never counted for very much. In an essay on Verga, D. H. Lawrence went so far as to imagine that "there probably wasn't a single cultivated person in Sicily, for he would have fled the place long ago." The Sicilian intellectuals are so widely dispersed and atomized that one may indeed believe that they don't exist.

So much for Sicily's reasonable and realistic Roman soul: an engrafted superstructure, a codified elaboration. But something must be said about the eternal dialogue between this Roman soul and the Arab soul, by far the more popular and whose traces appear in the fables and tales found among the people, in the stories that have come down to us in dialect. The Arab soul is a wellspring of fantastic, surreal creativity, replete with resurgences of the *Thousand and One Nights*. Its most concentrated expression is in the character of Giufà, the typical Sicilian-Arabic hero, with his involuntary mischievousness: it's always the events that are mischievous, not Giufà himself. This half-wit, socially classified as such, and who, because of his very stupidity finds himself having to face pernicious situations from which in the end he emerges unscathed through want of cunning, does not—contrary to what you might suppose—belong to the peasant world. He is instead the typical inhabitant of an oriental city, a stevedore, a porter, one of those fellows always hanging about the edges of marketplaces. Perfectly mindless of the consequences of his actions, he is surrounded by a kind of halo, an aura like the one that envelopes a madman.

Here's a Giufà episode: weary of being persecuted by flies, and knowing that one must apply to a judge in order to obtain redress, Giufà betakes himself to a noble magistrate, who tells him: "My son, it is very simple. As soon as you see a fly, swat it." At that selfsame instant a fly lands daintily on the judge's cheek. Giufà's reaction is immediate: he springs forward and administers a ringing slap to the imprudent Solomon's face. The judge protests. Giufà replies: "But it was you, Signor Judge, who bade me kill them!"

Giufà the innocent has a precise function: to exercise a social vendetta against a representative of authority. He kills the fly and slaps the judge at the same time; absolutely irresponsible, he can't be prosecuted; revealer of the ridiculous, he evokes laughter, and with impunity. But his acts are solitary ones. Giufà never participates in a collective *beffa*, in the organized pranks that are part of the Tuscan tradition. He is always and forever completely alone.

Sicilian songs, too, are for solo singers; the tradition of the choral song doesn't exist here. Is it the eternal isolation of the islander? The individualistic fatalism that comes to us precisely from our Arab soul? Whatever the reason, our insecurity and fear of tomorrow are such that we ignore the future tense of verbs. We never say, "Tomorrow I will go to the country." We say, "*Dumani, vaju in compagna*"—tomorrow I am going to the country. We speak of the future only in the present tense. So when I am questioned about the native pessimism of the Sicilians, I feel like saying, "How can you fail to be pessimistic in a country where the future tense of verbs doesn't exist?"

But let's come back to solitude. Among us the idea is deeply rooted that in order to be yourself completely, you need to be alone; that solitude is the place where you "recover" yourself; that other people divide us, splinter us, multiply us (O Pirandello!); that with other people you can't be a living being, but only a character; and that to earn existence as a living being, you need to sneak away to solitude, you need to be a *uomo solo,* as Pirandello says in *One, None, and a Hundred Thousand*: "Solitude is never with you," he writes; "it is always without you, and possible only in an alien environment: a place or a person of whatever sort, for whom you are a total stranger, so that your will and your feelings remain suspended in an anguishing uncertainty, and every affirmation of yourself having ceased, there ceases the very intimacy of your consciousness. True solitude is in a place that lives for itself and, for us, no longer has a voice, and in which the stranger is you." There's one flaw in all of this. When you're alone, you're fatally in agreement with the world, and you don't even think of transforming it, improving it, or destroying it. You adjust to it such as it is!

Some people will see a contradiction between this desire for solitude—with the rejection of commitment it breeds—and the Sicilian's demand that his rights be respected. What is one to answer other than that the Sicilian is a product of his history? Is it his fault that he's never decided anything for himself, that other people have always acted for him, in his stead... Romans, Byzantines, Piedmontese? The only times the Sicilian has decided things on his own and resigned himself to making history on his own, he's been miserably mistaken: thus did the Sicilian Vespers come about, which slammed the door on France only to open it to Spain. If there were hundreds of thousands of reasons to produce those Vespers, and if a true problem of liberty lay at their origin, as Dante said, they nevertheless remain a fundamental error of judgment. In Sicily we've always been invaded and swindled by our conquerors, and when we haven't been invaded, it's sometimes been even worse. Just recall the fact that Sicily remained untouched by the Napoleonic conquests, which, thanks to the passage of the imperial armies, always left behind some trace of civilization—the Code Napoléon, for example.

Likewise, it was a disaster for us when the Bourbon court took refuge on the island under British protection, the single beneficent result of their presence being to stimulate a local industry, favoring the ascent of the Florio family: in the shipyards, the wine industry, canning, ceramics, etc. They were fragile conquests, however, which the Sicilian nobility hastened to spoil by fixing their eyes on the Florios, marrying the Florios, squandering the Florio revenues. But the coup de grace was delivered by the leaders of Northern industry, who found it intolerable that small-time parvenus from the South could become great industrialists. And by means of the loans and mortgages of the Commercial Bank, the Northerners devoured the fortunes of the Sicilian bourgeoisie. One must understand that Italian unity was able to come about only thanks to the following tacit pact: the South was to remain agricultural, the supplier of manual labor; only the North had the right to enrich itself and to become industrialized. Anybody who tampered with this equilibrium was to be eliminated; and that is how the Genoa-Milan-Turin industrial triangle made its financial and economic fortune from the Mezzogiorno. In this respect the story of the Florios is exemplary. Their story is the exact opposite of a tale from Balzac; marrying the offspring of nobility, these bourgeois lost their profits and wrote finis to their entrepreneurial destiny.

The Sicilian nobility resembles no other, in either the historical or the sociological sense. In the first place, because it was easy to come by a title under the Bourbons, and even under the Spanish. A writer of the seventeenth century states that to have a title, it was not necessary that "your father have never worked with his hands," it sufficed that you were a practitioner of *concavalli*, that is, that you knew something of horsemanship. It was a modest requirement, you'll admit. And one can guess what followed from it: the sole criterion of nobility became inactivity, whether intellectual or manual. Well, starting in the fifteenth century, this rather special nobility begins to abandon its castles, its lands and villages, and moves to the city, in particular to Palermo; and it loses interest in its fiefs, returning there only for vacations, as a reading of *The Leopard* will confirm. The first great crisis of the Sicilian aristocracy can be traced back to this epoch. And prior to then? About the times before then not a great deal is known; they are spoken of as a golden age, but how much basis is there to the claim?

Undoubtedly a city like Palermo has known its moments of

splendor, especially from the viewpoint of urban planning, when under the viceregency of the duke of Maqueda the city was split by the two rectilinear arteries that still divide it today; and when a genuine ruling class, made up of the last vestiges of the aristocracy, conferred upon Palermo a "liberty"-style physiognomy that derived directly from the European capital where this class had squandered its last resources—that is, Paris. Yet I don't have the slightest impression that Sicily ever knew any "golden age" followed by a period of decadence. In our country decadence is not a function of declining economic circumstances, but a permanent fact. It has always existed. All those who have landed on the island have pillaged what there was to pillage: the Romans began by cutting down every tree in sight, then this continued with the Spanish and the Piedmontese. When they called Sicily the "Breadbasket of the Empire," they didn't mean that it was a rich country, but that it represented an opportunity for systematic pillaging. Why? Because an island in the heart of the Mediterranean—that sea where for centuries the entire history of the world had taken place—cannot be anything else but a land for conquest and devastation. But, irony of fate, this island of a thousand invasions has held apart from the history that makes great peoples and great civilizations: it did not know the iron straitjacket of Napoleonic armies, nor the resistance to fascism like the rest of the Mezzogiorno and especially northern Italy. Here we didn't feel Mussolini's fall because we had never had a very clear view of his rise to power, and we passed from the Duce's administration to Uncle Sam's without any transition whatsoever. Not to have known those moments of transition, and therefore of rupture, was a terrible loss that still affects us today; all we lived through were gelatinous experiences which were hardly incentives to revolt or to revolution.

The very particular viscosity of Sicilian history is owing

also to the fact that we here have always placed our hopes in changes coming from outside and from above: every time a viceroy left Palermo, they danced for joy in every quarter of the city, because people believed that the next ruler would be better than his predecessor and that now things would *really* change. Nobody, however, thought of overturning the institution itself; the populace was educated to this idea of change descending from on high.

Of all the dominations that have come to us from abroad during the modern epoch, the one that best corresponded to Sicilian mentality was the Spanish domination. It was imposed, of course, but it suited us so well from an esthetic point of view! With their love for splendor, for richness and for festivity, with their fondness for wastefulness and for ostentatious expense, their leaning toward the grandiose and toward pomp, the Spanish put us at ease: we loved showiness even more than they did. Indeed, the term *spagnolesco* more befits Sicilians than Spaniards. Just one false note, if I may put it that way, in this Sicilian-Spanish connivence: in this festival the Spanish participated as masters, while the Sicilians enjoyed it as slaves.

In the grandiloquent hospitality that characterizes us, one can also discern the desire to show ourselves such as we are not, to elevate ourselves to the level of interlocutor or host, to present the best possible image of ourselves, even were it very far from the truth. This has nothing to do with generosity, which is gratuitous and does not seek to counterfeit appearances. Rather, it's a matter of amour propre, or, as La Rochefoucauld said, of self-love. "Whatever the finds that have been made upon the lands of amour propre, there yet remain numerous unknown regions to discover." La Rochefoucauld was talking about other forms and other manifestations of amour propre, of course; yet his use of the term "regions" seems to me highly suggestive: might not

Sicily be one of them? Among us an amour propre that is inseparable from our passion for "having"—the love we have for *roba*, meaning "stuff," as Giovanni Verga used to say. This *roba*, which can be land, a house, crockery, linens, livestock, provisions, seems only accidentally the source of some profit; one doesn't *use* it, one *leaves* it behind when one dies; it is bound up with feelings one nourishes for one's family, with one's apprehensions regarding the family's future and about the presence of death. The wealthier we grow, the greater grows the quantity of goods we'll leave when we die, and the greater and more amplified that death becomes. The rhythm of accumulation as rhythm of death ... Brancati, too, dwelt upon this apprehension about the future, this feeling of insecurity Sicilians have. An historic insecurity that invests affections and material belongings to an obsessive degree. Among us it's the ordinary thing for an everyday matter of a shared wall between two pieces of property, or of a right of way, to pass out of the hands of the land-registry expert into those of a ballistics expert—not because of low greed but out of an as it were preventive apprehensiveness. The land under the sun is never secure, misfortunes, or the neighbors, can gnaw it away, better therefore to protect it ahead of time, in the same way it is better to protect the family members by keeping them close under one's wing. What can actually happen to the person who leaves the house, even temporarily? Well, such persons can be robbed, raped, brutalized; they can lose their honor, even their lives. The Sicilian experiences the entire gamut of these feelings under the obsessive colors of apprehension.

But let's return to Spain and its influence on Sicily, which seems to me notable, even if we know almost nothing about the relationship between Spanish culture and Sicilian culture. You sense that the literate Sicilian was bilingual, that he knew Spanish as well as Sicilian. In Cervantes, who lived in

Messina, we can find hints of Sicily; we are forever noting the Spanish expressions that linger on in our speech; along with Americo Castro we do not hesitate to see in *Don Quixote* the matrix of the Pirandellian game the author plays with his character. However on the cultural plane we know nothing of any great weight. No one in Spain seems to have been interested in the reality of the Sicilian land. When Europeans begin to travel, the Germans, the English, and the French show up here; not, however, the Spanish. They have no interest in us at all. They seem to have felt greater fondness for any given region of South America than for the island of Sicily that was once actually theirs.

I never stop asking myself the reason for this ignorance on the part of the Spanish, and, more generally, about the singular destiny of my land which seems to evade history even when it is being raped by that very history. I think of these lines by Giuseppe Tomasi, prince of Lampedusa, in *The Leopard*—lines that point, assuredly, in a conservative direction, but with which I would tend to agree: " 'Do you really think, Chevalley,' " says Don Fabrizio, " 'that you're the first to try to channel Sicily into the flow of universal history? Who knows how many Muslim imams, how many of King Roger's knights, how many Swabian scribes, how many Angevin barons, how many of His Most Catholic Majesty's jurists have envisioned that same noble lunacy? And how many Spanish viceroys, those reform-minded functionaries of Charles III? And who now knows what became of them? Sicily has preferred to sleep in spite of their innovations.' "

It's true, reforms generally lead to nothing here. In these conditions I do not believe that a very great future lies ahead for Sicily. Paradoxically, you could say that only an enormous energy crisis could bring something new to Sicily, spurring a massive return to the land, an economic system oriented less toward industry and more toward agriculture, a renewed interest in producing instead of consuming. Sicily's problems are those of Italy, and I don't think it's possible to resolve them unless the ensemble of Italian problems are resolved at the same time. Unfortunately, it looks to me as though Italy has never been so anti-South as it is today, it thinks of nothing but manufacturing cars and building highway to drive those cars on; so now we have the Messina-Catania autostrada. Superb. And deserted—because it was costly to build, and pointless. If Italy does not exert itself to calm the anxieties of the Mezzogiorno, it will continue to "pump" a little more of the South up towards the North every day and to contaminate itself, it will absorb a little more Southern mentality, it will progressively "Sicilianize" itself. And so it is indeed that "the palm-tree line" mounts a few centimeters every year, inexorably, from the Straits of Messina towards the border with Austria.

Among the other great myths that the Sicilian mind has been or is yet stocked with is the myth of France. For the popular masses, France first represented a negative myth, arising from the episode of the Sicilian Vespers and continuing through the eighteenth century: one employed the word *France* to signify *hunger*, an allusion to the French of Charles of Anjou, who contented themselves with allowing Sicily to starve to death. For the aristocratic or cultivated classes, however, France—probably beginning around the seventeenth century, when the French polemic with Spain deepened—, France began to represent a positive myth. It's during the epoch of the Enlightenment that you see literary men taking the French Rationalists as their model. If you consult the customs and police records, you'll notice that the importation of French books is astonishing: Rousseau, Voltaire, *L'Encyclopédie*, Montesquieu (the favorite of the aristocrats). Stendhal would later say that French books sold poorly in Italy, except for Sicily, where every worthwhile book sold at least a hundred copies. Then, after the 1820 riots, this relationship with France became more stable and concrete, also because numerous Sicilians sought refuge as exiles in Paris.

Such was the importance of the French myth that the first true Sicilian narrator, when he wrote his first book, chose to write it in French: Michele Palmieri de Miccicché, author of two volumes of memoirs that were printed in Paris and earned praise from Stendhal and Alexandre Dumas. Let us not forget, incidentally, that numerous Stendhalian episodes come straight out of Palmieri! There were other writers, too, who wrote directly in French, among them Baron Aceto, the author in 1812 of a history of Sicily, and the Canon Gambini, who left the island during the Napoleonic period and was one of the translators of the Code into Italian. Finally, there is one basic work of romantic historiography—and one of the most alive, at least where it evokes Sicilian history—which would never have existed if the author, forced into exile, hadn't been able to avail himself of all the materials the Parisian libraries could provide. I refer to Michele Amari's *Histoire des Musulmans de Sicile*. Here in Palermo, unfortunately, there is not a document to be found on the Arab period in Sicily.

This tradition continues with—for example—Emanuele Navarro della Miraglia, who left for Paris after 1860. He, too, wrote a book in French, called *Ces messieurs et ces dames*, and he unfailingly kept his Sicilian friends apprised of the French literary movements and writers of the period. Navarro probably established the connection between French naturalism and the three Sicilian writers who identified themselves with it: Capuana, Verga, and De Roberto. It is certain that they worked together a great deal. Capuana and De Roberto subsequently turned out to be extremely well-informed and acute critics of French literature. They say that Navarro was one of George Sand's last friends, which set a lot of tongues wagging in Sicily, but I've never been able to find any trace of this story, not even in the Goncourts' *Journal*. Upon his Parisian sojourn Navarro wrote a book entitled *Macchiette parigine* (Parisian Sketches), done in a very lively style; it includes subtle assessments of Stendhal (in those days very little read outside of France) and of the majority of the epoch's writers.

In this list of Francophile men of letters we musn't neglect Nino Savarese, a Catholic writer animated by a great passion for Voltaire; Antonio Bruno, who translated the French Symbolists into Italian; and Luca Pignato and Vann'Antò (Giovanni Antonio di Giacomo), who, thanks to his translations, introduced Mallarmé into Italy. For my part I retain a marvelous memory of Luca Pignato, a professor of philosophy in Caltanissetta and a discerning connoisseur of French literature, who had us read works of which few persons had got wind. Thanks to him, we who are now close to sixty were exposed to Mallarmé's *L'Après-midi d'un faune*, Joyce's *Ulysses* in Valery Larbaud's translation, and all the Parnassians. Among Pignato's students were Giuseppe Alesi, today the editor of the *Enciclopedia italiana*. And Pompeo Colajanni, the famous communist senator and former partisan commander in Piedmont. Caltanisetta, in those years between 1935 and 1940, was a little Athens—if only because in that period of what Benedetto Croce called *onagrocrazia*—meaning the rule of donkeys—a young person like myself could encounter there such teachers as Luca Pignato, the Protestant poet Calogero Bonavia, Father Lamantia, Aurelio Navarria, the specialist in Verga, and Vitaliano Brancati. Literally raised on French literature, devoted to Chateaubrand and Stendhal (and, I might add, if in 1935, the year that Stendhal had prophesized he would be read, it was easy to fall in love with the author of *The Charterhouse of Parma*, this hardly applied to Chateaubriand), Brancati represents the summit of the pro-

French tradition in Sicily. For my own part I was rather late to come to Chateaubriand, sollicited by Brancati's anthology, and more recently by Maurice Nadeau, who told me that I had the look of a reader of Chateaubriand. I consider him an author who is still to be discovered and admired: those pages that have to do with Waterloo—one of the most wonderful confessions a man can make. Chateaubriand tells how he finds himself praying for Napoleon even as he stands in the other camp. I envy him his pitiless way of speaking about himself, that secret he possesses for recognizing that he has led the wrong life. Chateaubriand is an expression of the French soul par excellence; it would be difficult, it seems to me, to be more French than he was, with his continual hovering between monarchy of divine right and the Bonapartist adventure.

On the whole, I think that the relationships between Sicilian culture and French literature (and, more generally, the French world) have been insufficiently examined. Let's take the case of Brancati himself: who has ever thought to study the resemblances between Brancati's *Bell'Antonio* and Stendhal's *Armance*?

Anyway, just as a French-oriented Sicilian literature was developing during the late eighteenth century, a new myth was taking hold on the island—the myth of an erotic France, not only mother to the arts, to arms, and to law—what one has always expected of France—, but mistress of those sexual relationships called free ones, freed of all restraints. The Sicilian aristocracy threw away the last of its fortunes on the myth of erotic Paris, sending its offspring to the capital to experience that impossible liberty which they had pursued in vain on the island. To live in elegance, in the fountainhead of fashion and fashions—Francophile snobbishness was such that for a certain number of years a magazine was published in French called *La Sicile illustrée*, a stylish cultural weekly that disappeared with the First World War. From my childhood I had always heard France spoken of as a refined, erotic country, full of elegant things and wonderfully beautiful products. Later on, the literary myth of France was superimposed on these memories. The first French writer I happened upon was Diderot, whose *Paradoxe du comédien* had been brought out in an inexpensive series by Sonzogno. I read this book without possessing any great knowledge of the world of the theater and actors. What fascinated me was something else entirely: the way it was written, the intelligence of its form, the vivacity of its style, the author's angle of attack.

What was my second French book? Paul-Louis Courier's *Pamphlets*. Then *Les Misérables*. An extraordinary experience for me. I consider that the meager amount of Christianity I was able to discover (and retain) in my life is owing more to *Les Misérables* than to the Church in all its pomps and its works. I would even venture to add that anybody who has missed the importance of *Les Misérables* in the forming of the individual and collective conscience of two or three generations can understand nothing about Europe.

These days I spend more time rereading than reading, and I reread Diderot. Which reminds me of one of the very odd commentaries a book of mine gave rise to: "Without a doubt Sciascia will someday end up looking like Diderot," that literary critic wrote rather scornfully. He never realized that this was the supreme compliment he had paid to a man who idolizes Diderot. Diderot: there is a writer whose greatness only grows and who deserves to be more widely admired, even in France, where he isn't yet fully appreciated. Moreover, anticipating this incomprehension, Diderot himself announced (in his letter "to later generations") that he would be understood in due course. In my view he'll end up being more important than Voltaire, for over and above his formal qualities he was able to distinguish what today they call "material culture" and to describe it with precision. I do not dare even to speak of *L'Encyclopédie*, that prodigy of human intelligence, that projection of the most grandiose of wills to knowledge!

On the other hand, I believe that Voltaire reposes right on the line—if such a thing exists—where writers aim at finishing. He's the very example of literary professionalism, a model writer. Clear, swift, concise, precise, intelligent, economical, ironic: that's Voltaire, everything that, for me, represents the key to writing and true craft. And who's the exact opposite of Jean-Jacques Rousseau. I speak of Rousseau because you can't speak of Voltaire without mentioning his worst enemy. Actually, Rousseau interests me very little. From the time I first read *Emile*, at the age of fourteen, it struck me as the book of someone who knows nothing about human nature. And when it comes to confessions, I'll take Saint Augustine's. Indeed it was not until much later on that I understood the reasons why I felt nothing if not hatred for Jean-Jacques Rousseau: that fondness he had for "isms," those murderous "isms" that freight his work; his so-called discovery of the "general interest"! Whereas democracy is the expression of an arithmetical will, that of the more numerous, of the majority, Rousseau believed he had discovered a "general will" which doesn't coincide with the law of the greater number, which can be the apanage of a few or of some while claiming to be the rightful interpreter of the will of all. In proclaiming that a part can take the place of the whole, in talking about the general will, Rousseau is at the source of the principal evils of our time.

From Rousseau to the French Revolution: it should surprise nobody that the "Hermit of Geneva" inspires me to talk about 1789. I did not learn about the French Revolution through books. They made fleeting references to it in school, of course, mostly to emphasize that the Revolution had given birth to Napoleon. No, my first inkling of the Revolution came from barbers' calendars and pictures painted on carts: in other words, for me its initial allure was purely esthetic. The cart-painters loved to depict Danton and Camille Desmoulins. Why was that? Because these painters copied the calendars, and the calendars, the precursors of modern comic strips, showed a marked preference for the sentimental histories of the heroes they portrayed. Thus Desmoulins and Danton, who had lived somewhat tumultuous sentimental lives, lent themselves wonderfully to these illustrated narratives.

Then—and I am still talking about my childhood—I came across a popular novel entitled *Il Fabbro del convento*, a translation of Ponson du Terrail's *Le Forgeron du convent*. Thus, my earliest notions of the French Revolution were totally novelistic and, what is more, based upon an abusive conception of revolutionaries, who were systematically presented as the bad guys. Not until I got to some other popular novels written by William Galt (a pseudonym of the Sicilian Luigi Natoli) did the Revolution appear to me in its true dimension, in its real nature. Thanks to Galt, I grasped its bearings upon Sicilian history, and from his *Beati Paoli* I borrowed the lawyer Francesco Paolo de Blasi, one of the heroes in my *The Council of Egypt*. Today I'm inclined to think that the French Revolution was the single great revolutionary event to have occurred in the whole world.

But I have strayed from my subject, which was the Sicilian's mentality. My point of departure was Cicero, who devoted a certain number of pages to the liking for controversy and for sophistry which he judged typically Sicilian, and I was wondering whether, essentially, there did not indeed exist a nature that was eternally Sicilian. But at the same time I am also convinced that a particular nature alone cannot serve to explain everything, and that one must have recourse to historic mechanisms. Thus the Sicilian's juridical passion must have been formed over the course of centuries, because he must have been obliged to reckon with a quantity of laws, with a quantity of elements from which privileges flowed. Sicily had become the land where special jurisdictions, or privileged courts, were most numerous. For example: the Monarchical Tribunal, to which any citizen involved in a dispute with the Roman Curia could turn whenever the issue had to do with articles of faith. Then there was the privileged court of the Inquisition: all the employees of the Inquisition, as well as their families—that is, all of this organization's "lay" agents, who numbered in the thousands in Sicily—enjoyed the privilege of being judged by the Inquisition itself, even if they had committed crimes under common law. Another special *forum*: the one known as "vicarial." In each community there was a vicarial court with its appropriate police, which judged crimes such as profanity, the nonobservance of fasts, and certain sexual transgressions (not all: adultery and homosexuality came within the purview of normal tribunals) such as the consummation of an amorous relationship with a woman during a period in which the Church advocated abstinence. And then there were the special *forums* for certain chivalric orders. The conflicts among these often antagonistic jurisdictions were unending. I may add that when the State tried to inject a little bit of order into the usurpations of public property, by for example claiming a prior right to certain domains, the average Sicilian found himself at sea. No wonder, then, that this mess produced a world of disputes, lawsuits, and polychrome jurisprudences, that the Sicilian became an expert on laws and rights of all sorts, and that there emerged a class of battle-hardened jurists, one of whose principal functions was to spread an essentially juridical culture everywhere, even among the poorer classes. At work underneath all that there may have been the aspiration to a true, not formalist, justice; an aspiration of which the Mafia, in the final analysis, would merely be one of the expressions.

If it's true that function creates the organ, let us say that this continual jurisprudential to-and-fro, which has kept the Sicilian immersed in a perpetual codified contest, has created in him a peculiar intelligence that I would define as "formal", an intelligence apt at grasping the weak points in an opposing argument and turning them to his advantage—his formal or material advantage. The form of discourse that distinguishes Pirandello's characters can also be seen as juridical or casuistical: Pirandello describes how feelings are sometimes got hold of by the mind, becoming purely cerebral. According to him, every kind of passion, whether it be for a woman or for an object, expresses itself at some point in terms of rights or in a purely procedural form. Following this line of thought, I would say that almost every "crime of honor" falls into the sphere of patrimonial rights. (These crimes have diminished today thanks to the law on divorce and the growing prevalence of marriage contracts based on the separation of property.)

In 1946 I attended two trials. At them the specific charge was "violation of the laws governing food control." Back then there were particularly rigorous laws concerning the harvesting of grain. Farmers were required to deliver their harvests over to state-controlled warehouses, keeping for their own personal use the equivalent of one-and-a-half quintals of wheat for each family member. Naturally the peasants held on to more than that, and whenever the police found out arrest was immediate, as was prosecution. At the time I was employed by the state granary, and it was in that capacity that I was obliged to participate in the two trials.

One trial concerned a peasant in whose house two or three extra quintals of grain had been found; the other, an archpriest who had managed to squirrel away fifteen quintals. The proceedings before the Agrigento tribunal were very swift. The peasant was condemned to two years in jail. The archpriest was absolved, because his lawyer managed to explain that there was nothing criminal in the act of setting wheat aside in order to distribute it later as alms to the poor and unfortunate, to the people who are in hospitals, for example. This first contact with the administration of justice was decisive for me. The absolving of the archpriest convinced me that in truth justice did not exist, and that in any event the day of privileged *forums* in Sicily had not yet come to an end.

IV. The Writer's Truth

MARCELLE PADOVANI. Which of your characters best represents you? Were you the dreadful boy in *The American Aunt* who is involved in smuggling cigarettes, who enjoys spitting on coins, who makes obscene noises with his lips during on-screen kisses at the movies, and who collects stray cartridges from American machine guns? Or were you that perfect little know-it-all of a child named Candido, who always eats with a good appetite, sleeps like an angel from the moment his head hits the pillow, and detests dangerous games? Or the policeman-moralist Rogas, who, over and above truth, loves "wild game, free-range chickens, country bread, wine, those relics from the golden age"? Perhaps you are Abbot Vella, that genial falsifier of chronicles and methodical impostor who asserts that "The work of the historian is an imbroglio... History doesn't exist," the while dedicating himself to pleasure and luxury? Or the lawyer De Blasi, agnostic and liberal, so consistent with himself that he becomes a conspirator capable of resisting the worst tortures, and who ends up symbolizing what is best in a human being? In any case, whether your heroes are policemen, professors, priests, or politicians, they all have something in common: they represent key parts in the functioning of society, the various knots and articulations of power.

* * *

LEONARDO SCIASCIA. The relationship I have with my characters is pretty simple, doubtless because I've never encountered a single one who created difficulties for me. For the most part, people I know from everyday life furnish me with the basic elements for each of my characters or for a historic character, to whom I may eventually attribute features borrowed from my contemporaries. I don't have a great creative imagination. My heroes are the exact opposite of Pirandello's: the distance between real life and the sheet of paper is minimal in their case, and the discrepancy is very slight; thus they're not characters who demand to exist in a book, but rather already existent beings who appear spontaneously on the page.

I don't see myself completely in any of them. But a part of me lives in each of them, not least because of the fact that I make them mine; I describe and I become responsible for them in the attempt to understand and penetrate inside them. So I'm partly a Mafia kingpin, partly a priest, partly a lawyer and partly an inquisitor—and here I'm limiting myself to the characters we might call negative. Naturally I see more of myself in the ones I love, in the characters we call positive.

MARCELLE PADOVANI. Why are priests so numerous in your work?

LEONARDO SCIASCIA. Because so many of the evils afflicting Italy come from them or through them, and then because I am susceptible to the fascination that revealed religion and Catholicism are able to exert, all the while feeling myself unable to penetrate inside it or accede to it. In this sense *One Way or Another* represented for me a way of squaring my accounts with a certain Church, a way of freeing myself from the attraction it exerts upon me and which shows me that in reality I am not much of a Sicilian. This religion always struck me as a safe harbor, a haven, a quiet beach upon which I wish

I were able to go to sleep, I who am nothing but an unbeliever. For her part, Sicily takes the opposite course: she is more or less refractory to religion; more or less impermeable to faith; knows more or less nothing of true belief. And it's too bad. For if religious peoples are capable of making religious revolutions, they also are able to bring about civil revolutions.

Religion deeply lived therefore represents for me the aspiration to find a center, a bliss, a total and totalizing vision of life. But religion is the aspiration to the contrary of peace, that is to say, to torment, to disquiet, to a perpetual searching. Naturally, one cannot accept a religion once and for all; one must live it day after day, in conflict with oneself and in the greatest pain. Nevertheless, all this anxiousness, these concerns—I see them turning about a very precise center, which is not belief in God but the certainty that everything does not end with the disappearance of the body, the idea that there is something *other* for whose sake we exist, and that our existence, painful and difficult, is not totally devoid of meaning, even beyond the few years of temporal life that are conceded to us.

During the last century, and particularly during ours, men have lived as if Dostoevsky's famous phrase—"God does not exist, therefore nothing is permitted"—had decreed the nonexistence of God once and for all, and had confirmed, oddly enough, that everything was permitted. But it's not possible to live without God and permit yourself everything; you can only live without him by permitting yourself nothing. Yes. For my part I believe that our epoch conceals a desperate although often subterranean search for God, I believe that terrorism is itself search for God, thirst for mysticism, need for that absolute that God can give. The trouble is that the terrorists have transferred this God-given absolute to the level of civic life, and consequently the various incarnations of violence simply represent the search for a purposeless religion.

MARCELLE PADOVANI. Your most recent hero is Aldo Moro, the political figure who was murdered by the Red Brigades. These Red Brigade terrorists, do you describe them too as religious men?

LEONARDO SCIASCIA. There is no difference between a member of the Red Brigades and an inquisitor in the time of the Spanish Inquisition, no more than there was between that inquisitor and a convinced Stalinist during the fifties. Malraux said that in his opinion Stalin's thinking was "statistical," and he was perfectly right. Stalin would think: "If I eliminate Tom, who knows Dick, who knows Harry, who knows a fascist, then there won't be any more fascists, I will have progressively got rid of them." The inquisitor too thought that in eliminating the one who had known the person who knew a heretic, he was suppressing the heresy. And the trials staged by the inquisitors were at least as complex as the trials under Stalin. It is inexact to say that they were satisfied with an apparent consensus and a public but purely formal recantation; no, the inquisitors truly desired the heretic's conversion; they wished to convince him that he had been on the path of wickedness but that there was still time to take the good one. Right to the very end the Inquisition tries to convince my hero Fra Diego La Matina that he is in error, but Fra Diego holds out. But in most cases people ended up persuading themselves that they had indeed been in error, exactly as in the course of Stalin's trials. The mechanism is identical. You begin with the following statement to the accused: "Independently of the fact that you did or did not commit this error, from the moment you are accused of having committed it, it is obvious that the confession of this error may at least serve to keep others from committing it." Then you end by convincing him that he really was in error. And in the course of those trials under Stalin they would say to the accused: "Maybe you didn't really conspire, but if you confess that you did, you will incite others to be vigilant, you will be useful to socialism."

As for "Red Brigade man," to use Pope Paul VI's expression, what goes on in his head is the same thing that goes on in the inquisitor's and in the Stalinist judge's. The Red Brigades created a power for themselves. From the moment they succeeded in sowing terror, in striking practically wherever they saw fit, they became a real power; and they have not the faintest doubt that this power will grow, and that it will end up being *the* power. Whence the kidnappings and the trials. Characteristic, wouldn't you say, that the Red Brigades also claimed they were trying Aldo Moro, present-day "inquisitee" examined on non-religious grounds. If the inquisitor believed he represented the entirety of the world of the faithful, and Stalin's judge the working class, the Red Brigades believe they are the representatives of the proletariat.

MARCELLE PADOVANI. But why do priests keep recurring in your work as if they too were the symbol of power, or else the indispensable mediators between power and God's people?

LEONARDO SCIASCIA. I've known two kinds of priests. First, the Sicilian priest, often ignorant or, when he wasn't, a good deal worse—that is, pleasure-loving, busily feathering his nest, and with an open mind. That's the priest produced by a society in which, in order that a poor family mount the rungs of social prestige, one of the sons has had to agree to wear the cassock. Charged with the task of boosting the social condition of his kin, their delegated promoter, he would undertake certain studies—summary studies—in the name of the whole family, and would resign himself to spreading the word of Christ even if he had not the least vocation. Chosen for the seminary, this young fellow remained aware that he was to "redeem" his family, and demonstrated an insatiable avidness for the goods of this world: he consumed enough for two, or for ten . He entered a rather numerous and rather protected corporation, which in addition enjoyed a series of special immunities—immunities that were particularly interesting in Sicily due to the existence of the Monarchical Tribunal, which removed the priests from the Roman Curia's judgment in all matters having to do with their priestly behavior, unless their errors bore upon dogma. This is the "ideal type" of Sicilian priest you find in our countryside.

The other type of priest, symbolized by Don Gaetano in *One Way or Another*, is the cultivated, well-read priest, who, I think, belongs more to French Catholic culture than Italian. To actually find Don Gaetano's equivalent in Italy—a cultivated, intelligent priest, a great lover of art and esthetics—you'd have to start looking among the cardinals.

MARCELLE PADOVANI. And the Zafer hermitage, where Don Gaetano celebrates his masses—is that also the fruit of your imagination?

LEONARDO SCIASCIA. On a height a little outside the place called Zafferana Etnea, a few kilometers from Catania, stands an "Emmaus inn," which is run by the Salesian Order. In summer a gathering is held there for the awarding of the Vitaliano Brancati Prize, and that is how I came to find myself there in August. I spent a good month there and I was witness to a series of rather disconcerting spiritual exercises that the Salesians' pupils were wont to perform. Odd pupils, I must say: almost all notables of the Christian Democrat Party. At the end of every day I would see them first march ahead and then march backwards in front of the inn, all the while reciting their rosary. It was around that incredible scene that I constructed *One Way or Another*.

MARCELLE PADOVANI. Could it be said that your characters are mediators, that they have been given a mission which is to induce the underlying population to accept the weight of the the ruling powers and the burden of poverty?

LEONARDO SCIASCIA. Perhaps the priests, but not the policemen. For me policemen simply incarnate the law, without which a society cannot live. What makes them unhappy is the failure of their efforts to apply this law. They are honest and strict, animated by good principles—the same principles that inspire every democratic state—but on a practical level they're reduced to impotence. In any case, my policemen are more like ideas than characters, more abstractions than realities. I've never met the equivalent of Inspector Rogas or Captain Bellodi, the hero of *The Day of the Owl*. I have doubtless gleaned a few features, a few elements, from those poor defenders of the law that I've happened to meet; but never an entire character.

MARCELLE PADOVANI. Leaving aside this fortuitous happening upon bits and pieces of characters, what is the general point of departure for your books? An item in the news, a political event, a document you have been shown? And how do you conduct your investigations, your research? Do you feel yourself a detective, a journalist, an historian?

LEONARDO SCIASCIA. Each of my books has a different point of departure. Let's take *Sicilian Uncles*. I was once at the Racalmuto station waiting for a train, and with a kind of indifferent passivity I was witnessing the arrival of groups of Sicilians who had emigrated to America and were coming back to visit their families. Rediscoveries, tears of joy, huggings, emotions! At exactly that moment somebody beside me muttered in a sarcastic tone: "And in less than a week they'll be at one another's throats." The observation jolted me awake, gave me the impetus to portray this epic return to the village birthplace: the jests at the "Americans'" expense, the jealousies, the scuffles arising from the generational and economic differences between those who had stayed at home and those who returned from America after twenty years.

The Death of Stalin originated in my friendship for an old communist who, after the publication of the Krushchev Report, went down every morning to the local Communist Party office to make sure that Stalin's portrait hadn't been removed. *Antimonio* was inspired by a passage in Malraux's *Man's Hope*, that particular episode at Guadalajara when a patrol of antifascist Italians clashed with a patrol of fascist Italians. This same episode was recounted to me by my lawyer who had been involved in it personally: as a fascist volunteer in the Spanish Civil War. A genuine volunteer, who had gone there out of conviction (when I knew him, he had become a Christian Democrat): the very opposite of the poor peasants and sulfur-miners who enlisted for money, to avoid dying of hunger.

The Day of the Owl was inspired by the Mafia's murder of the Syndicalist-Communist Miraglia, at Sciacca. *The Council of Egypt* was written in place of another book: I wanted to chronicle the massacre of the supposed Jacobins that took place in Caltagirone at the end of the eighteenth century, and I had begun to collect documents on the subject. While I went through Domenico Scinà's literary history of Sicily, sifted the material that remained in the archives, and then read the Marchese di Villabianca's Chronicles, I found myself drawn to the figure of the Abbot Vella. Then, in the same documents that I used for *The Council of Egypt*, I came upon another character, who after that never left my mind and who inhabits me yet, Fra Diego la Matina, who furnished the starting point for *The Death of the Inquisitor*, my favorite of all my books.

On the other hand, *A Man's Blessing* is the product of a deliberate decision. I had said to myself that I wanted to write an account of an historical failure, the failure of the center-left coalition. Starting in 1964, the center-left as a government formula had brought the Socialist Party into a partnership with the Christian Democrats for the management of the country's affairs. But after having raised so many hopes among the population, the coalition left us all sunk in despair. The event represented by this partnership, which in effect ought to have provoked a radical change in Italian political life, had been yet another time engulfed in the eternal immutability of eternal Italian fascism. The book, however, was interpreted as a story of the Mafia.

I hadn't meant to start on a systematic review of the genesis of each of my books or stories, but I would like to give two further examples. First, *The Mystery of Majorana*. For a long time I had been fascinated by the renunciation of this very young and very illustrious Italian physicist on the eve of the Second World War; he belonged to Fermi's school, he had certainly discovered something important when, in 1938, he suddenly decided to disappear. I had already assembled a certain number of documents regarding him—the letters to his family, what could be found at the National Archives in Rome—but I wasn't thinking about starting to write. Then I took part in a television broadcast on the thirtieth anniversary of the end of the war, along with Alberto Moravia and the physicist Emilio Segrè. When they showed us a film clip of the first atomic bomb exploding, I was struck by Segrè's serenity, his tranquil demeanor. Then I thought once more of

Majorana, the tormented, uncertain, brilliant young physicist, he who had dreaded the consequences of his discoveries. Having, as I believe, discovered the secret of the atomic bomb, and having intuited the consequences of nuclear fission, he had preferred to disappear. I tried to find out where he was hiding, whether he was dead, whether he had committed suicide; I went to inquire at a monastery near Naples. But Majorana had staged his disappearance so effectively that no trace of his person remained.

As for *Equal Danger*, it originated in the same way as *A Man's Blessing*. I was intending to write a book on the Italian political situation, even on the international one, but the project remained pretty vague and I dragged along without making any real headway. For some fun, I set about writing a detective thriller: the story of a husband unjustly accused of trying to poison his wife, and out of all this *Equal Danger* emerged, an account of that social desertification which was then only in its beginning stages in Italy.

Then there's *Candido*, and the other books... At bottom, all my books are nothing but the story of a series of disappointments: historical and personal, past and present, with those of the past seen in the light of those of the present, and vice versa.

MARCELLE PADOVANI. Without expecting to resolve the problem of inspiration, I'd still very much like to know how you work, in a concrete sense—for example, whether for you there are certain optimal technical conditions for the creation of a book, whether the actual work of writing is something you experience as fatiguing effort, as pleasure, as an amusement, as the pursuit of a trade. You say in connection with *Candido* that at the outset you were afraid of boring the reader; in connection with *Equal Danger*, that you started it "for some fun." In any case, your books give the impression that they were written with the reader in mind, that they deliberately place themselves on the side of those who will read them.

LEONARDO SCIASCIA. I write every day, I take notes, I keep a kind of diary. But I write books only in the summer, when I'm living in the country. By now it's an unchanging ritual. When the idea for a book begins to take hold of me, I lovingly cultivate it for an entire year, sometimes two. I scrupulously read everything that's been written on the subject, I do research, I go and talk to people, and I jot down in my notebooks the points that seem most important to me, or sometimes simple annotations or vague details whose potential future significance I've intuited. Then I let my imagination go to work, and under its influence the subject ripens. Summer comes around; the whole family moves to Racalmuto, and finally I begin to write.

I write two or three pages a day, no more—very slowly, making few corrections and without ever rewriting—from seven in the morning until eleven o'clock or noon. I have the feeling, and perhaps it's rather silly, I have the feeling I have achieved ideal conditions for writing, and that in part is how I account for the pleasure I experience in drafting my books. I have noticed, moreover, that the books that I have most enjoyed writing are the same ones that have had the most success with the public. When I'm not having a good time, my book isn't coming along well; when I realize that I am about to become annoyed or exhausted by writing, I prefer to stop, to defer things until tomorrow or, if I am going to continue, to work only on what proves enjoyable. I write for four or five hours a day, without it tiring me at all—although I may feel tired afterward—and after these intense hours spent at my desk I feel the need to reimmerse myself in "civilian life," to see people, to chat with them.

* * *

MARCELLE PADOVANI. Here we come back to the theme of professionalism and craft. It seems to me that in your work these things strike one immediately. There's a great technical mastery that enables you to exploit every last bit of the reader's interest, a stylistic skill, a skill in construction that demonstrate just how well you know your "trade."

LEONARDO SCIASCIA. First of all, I'd like to say something about pleasure and amusement. At the moment I am in the midst of reading a certain number of Italian writers, and I'm forced to recognize that what they are doing does not entertain them any more than it entertains the reader; they are unable to conceal the exertion and boredom they feel when writing. It's a terrible impression. You sense that the writer sits himself down at his desk and says, "I absolutely have to write this damned book, so let's be done with it as soon as possible." Which accounts for the gaps, the obscure points, the incomprehensibilities, the empty phrases, and above all the development, through fantastic boredom, of a kind of scriptural paranoia. Behind all this are attitudes that I cannot understand; I'm tempted to send a little note to some of these authors: "But why the devil write? Don't subject yourself to this pain, this suffering, this torture." This also reveals the extent to which I feel myself a dilettante in comparison to these lovers of forced labor, a dilettante in the literal sense of the term, that is: "one who takes *diletto*, or delight."

But indeed yes, in writing I am pursuing a trade, and it is a trade I pursue seriously. They sell good shoes in the shops nowadays, better still, they are improving the quality of shoes all the time; why not sell good books to people? I don't mean to say that when I am writing I am thinking about nothing but my reader, that I am a victim of my eventual reader; actually, I think mostly of myself—or, to be more exact, of the reader as another me—and I consider it the worst hypocrisy to dare to say, for example, that "I am a writer who writes for the workers." Even if the working class reads books, and maybe even *my* books, I don't feel in the least authorized to say that I write for it. I write for me and for other me's: this must be seen as a fundamental ethical principle.

MARCELLE PADOVANI. But why would it be more moral to write for yourself rather than for others?

LEONARDO SCIASCIA. Because one cannot trifle with oneself. Because every one of us takes himself so seriously and feels regarding himself such respect that that constitutes the best of all possible commitments in favor of honesty. And finally, to write for yourself is a guarantee that you won't make the reader waste his time. In short, and to return to my own case, let's just say that I write about myself, for myself, and sometimes against myself.

By way of example let us take this Sicilian reality in which I live. I disapprove of and condemn many of its elements, but they are part of my life, I live them, with pain and from the inside; my "Sicilian being" suffers unspeakably from the game of Aunt Sally I subject myself to. When I denounce the Mafia I suffer at the same time; the residues of *sentire mafioso*, in me as in all Sicilians, are still there. Thus in struggling against the Mafia, I struggle against myself and it hurts. The same thing where the subject is Sicilian women: into my way of describing and condemning them there also enters a condemnation of myself. I suffer over *having* to discuss the Sicilian woman in her historic role—that is, as a negative element in the evolution of the island's society—; in her matriarchal function, stifling and conservative, such as it weighed upon our grandfathers and fathers, and such as it can still weigh today. But at the same moment I judge her, I feel responsible for her condition, atavistically responsible.

* * *

MARCELLE PADOVANI. What personal or historical developments does your work bear witness to? You seem to have progressed from the provincial chronicle, indeed, the village chronicle, to literary criticism, to the detective novel, and then on to ancient and contemporary history, not omitting the philosophical tale, of which the best illustration is your *Candido*. Is there a history underlying your choice of different genres? Do your books bear the mark of the various stages you've passed through as a human being?

LEONARDO SCIASCIA. No, there's no history. I mean there's no order, progress, design. There are the interests of the moment. There is the unpredictable nature of life. Every time I think I know what I am going to write tomorrow, behold! I set to work at the urging of considerations contrary to those which had been preoccupying me up to that moment. For example, once I was asked to write an opening address for a musical conference devoted to *I vespri siciliani*. I'm not a devotee of music, and I rarely listen to it: Mozart, Rossini, a little Verdi, Bizet's *Carmen*. But the request was so strange, so unexpected, that for a month I busied myself with Verdi's opera, even going to Parma to see what I could find at the Verdi Institute.

MARCELLE PADOVANI. What books are left for you to write? Or better, what are the themes that remain close to your heart and that you haven't yet had the occasion to address?

LEONARDO SCIASCIA. There are so many—were I to enumerate them I would spare myself from books that I shall never succeed in writing.

MARCELLE PADOVANI. As you see it, what is the hierarchical order of your work? Sometimes, although rarely, you let slip a judgment on your output. In an introduction to *Le parrochie de Regalpetra* you say: "I must admit that, having begun to publish my work after the age of thirty, I no longer experience problems of expression, of form, other than those concerning the need to give to the known a more rational order than to the knowable, and to document and narrate with good technique (and that, for instance, is why it's more pressing for me to follow the evolution of the detective novel than the development of esthetic theories)." Then you speak of *The Death of the Inquisitor* as "the book that I value most among all those that I've written." It is, you add, "an unfinished book that I will never finish, which I am still tempted to rewrite and never do, waiting to discover something new: a new document, a new revelation, a clue . . ." And further on: "I have worked on this book with more commitment and passion than any other." Why is *The Death of the Inquisitor* so important to you?

LEONARDO SCIASCIA. I can only repeat my preference and the reasons for it that you have just stated. My other books no longer interest me. Once they're written, it's as though they do not belong to me anymore. I don't reread them, I don't think about them. And, what's more, this is as it should be: why should I waste time with things already done, already experienced? I have other things to do, to experience. *The Death of the Inquisitor* is an unfinished book, waiting to be completed. I love it *quia imperfectum*.

MARCELLE PADOVANI. The language you use. Dense and chiseled, efficient and transparent, finely wrought, your sentences have sometimes been described as "Jansenist." Yet we're talking about an altogether modern, very cinematographic prose. By what path did you reach this style?

* * *

LEONARDO SCIASCIA. I think my writing experience is very complex, even if it has led to simple results. For a long time I took as my model the writers who contributed to *La Ronda*, a magazine published during the twenties and which made constant reference to the criteria of order, clarity, and simplicity. Then my ideal became Bruno Barilli, whose usual activity as a music critic didn't stop him from setting down accounts of his travels, which abounded in rapid, highly detailed descriptions. When I went to school I wrote like Barilli, used whole sentences that were his—brief, staccato sentences—to the point of caricature. Then there was Manzoni. If I were asked to which line of writers I belong, and if in my reply I had to limit myself to a single name, I would without any doubt advance that of Manzoni. Manzoni, I may add, along with being the best Italian writer is also the one that envelops French literature.

MARCELLE PADOVANI. Has your development entailed some kind of rupture with Sicily, with Sicily from the standpoint of dialect, literary experience, and manner of expression?

LEONARDO SCIASCIA. As I wrote in my preface to *Parrocchie*, style has never presented any problems for me; my personal quality of writing came to me naturally, so to speak. When I chance to reread a passage from one of my books, I notice that my syntax has moved steadily away from that of dialect, that my use of "Sicilianisms" has become more rare nowadays, that *Parrocchie* is full of dialect while *One Way or Another* is devoid of it; but I notice as well that the whole process has gone forward in a natural way. Since I distanced myself psychologically, intellectually, and sentimentally from Sicilian life, was it not to be expected that I would likewise move away from the syntax that typifies the island? In any case, this moving away has never made me feel inwardly torn, any more than the writer's task has constituted a kind of suffering for me. Here I am reminded of Buffon's famous phrase, which is so blindingly true: "The style is the man," he used to say. And the man grows, matures, is transformed; it is the same with style.

MARCELLE PADOVANI. Can one still say that you are a Sicilian writer? And in what sense?

LEONARDO SCIASCIA. There has been a progressive broadening of my horizons, and little by little I have no longer felt myself a Sicilian, or at least only a Sicilian. Rather, I am an Italian writer who is deeply familiar with the reality of Sicily, and who remains convinced that Sicily presents a synthesis of so many problems, so many contradictions—and not only Italian but European ones—that it constitutes a metaphor for the modern world. Given these conditions, am I still a Sicilian writer? And what is a writer anyway? For my part, I maintain that the writer is a man who takes pleasure in the truth and in the fact of telling the truth, and who finds fulfillment in a life lived as an instrument of writing. It is always with the greatest joy that I have sat down at my working table, persuaded as I have been that writing constitutes a kind of redoubling of the pleasure of living, and I have never written—except on very exceptional occasions—either under pressure exerted by someone else or from duty or with the feeling that what I am doing is drudgery.

MARCELLE PADOVANI. Writing is a diversion?

LEONARDO SCIASCIA. In a certain sense, it is. But to have chosen some sort of serious work, following the common definition of the term, would have meant, for example, remaining a clerk in an office or a teacher. To be quite honest, what I do as a writer cannot be considered work, for work means suffering, daily pain, gritting one's teeth and bearing it. Instead all I do is look for documentation, I hang about in libraries, double-check facts, conduct interviews, outline projects. Objectively, you could call it work, but subjectively, no: where's the pain in all of this? If I am able to accomplish something that from society's point of view is akin to work because it involves a certain moral tension, and the use of the methods of the policeman, the archivist, or the journalist (with their complement of often fruitless investigations and their inevitable failures) may it be said that from my personal point of view that constitutes a strain? Thus the months that I pass, often in wintertime, without writing a thing, without working in a regular manner on a definite project, for me represent periods full of fatigue, nervous exhaustion, and useless tension. At the moment, for example, I feel empty, listless—*crevé*, as they say in Paris—because I haven't written anything this year, and I dream, as of a happy vacation, of the moment when I'll set out for the country, where I'll begin to put my assembled materials in order, reread my notes, and where I'll feel the blessed instant of the alchemy of writing approaching. In those moments I feel that things will arrange themselves of their own accord, that their internal order will soon appear, that I'll rapidly discern the crux of my enterprise, that I'll begin to write swiftly, and that I'll be happy, relaxed, organized.

MARCELLE PADOVANI. You give the impression that what you are actually doing is playing with the meaning of the word *work*: you begin by defining it as pain and difficulty, and then, observing that so far as you are concerned writing does not entail anything bothersome, you say that as a writer you are not engaged in work. But the question can be posed in these terms: are you a professional or an occasional dilettante?

* * *

LEONARDO SCIASCIA. With my technique, and with the discipline I have imposed on myself, I could in theory write a book every six months. And then, true enough, I would not enjoy myself at all. I'd like to be very clear on this dimension of enjoyment—it's important. For example, I've never tried to rewrite one of my books, to run it through the mill a second, a third time. The only thing of mine that I've ever rewritten was the story entitled "Giufà." Yes, it's better written in the second version than the first, it's more pleasing and fluent. But if I was able to rewrite it that is because it is only four or five pages long. What hell it would have been if it had run to two or three hundred pages! Oh yes, put me down as a dilettante, one with the potential of becoming a professional.

MARCELLE PADOVANI. In any case, one can only say, as one looks at the record, that a magical rapport has come into being between the things you write, the things you seem to want to say, and what those things may be in reality.

LEONARDO SCIASCIA. I wouldn't be able to analyze the phenomenon, although it is one that I deeply sense. In a word, I don't understand obscure writers, those who do not succeed in saying what they think, what they want or what they dream of, those who are so tormented that their writing is unreadable. There shouldn't, though, in my view, be anything mysterious about this relationship between saying, thinking, and getting the thing down. In effect, however, the result may be better or worse depending on the circumstances. As regards myself I can only say that, yes, sometimes one manages to express one's thoughts particularly well, and with maximum clarity. When I have the impression that this has happened it gives me a feeling of security, of a sound and almost limpid relationship with reality. Then I'm convinced that there's nothing

I can't communicate to my fellow men; I'm persuaded that the sum of my experience, my knowledge, and my sensations is profoundly transmissible. At times I even find myself thinking—like that character in Borges—that "if I were in conditions of absolute security and solitude and could concentrate myself absolutely on the idea of God, then I would succeed in expressing this idea," and thus finally be God.

So many things, at a certain moment, converge to produce a writer! Innate elements, historical intersectings, economic factors. For example, without the solfataras—without the presence and weight of the sulfur mines—I believe that western Sicily, the home of Pirandello, Rosso di San Secondo, Nino Savarese, Francesco Lanza, and myself, would never have produced any writers. The sulfur deposits represent the opening of a great window upon the world, a great moment in the Sicilian's waking to consciousness. Into that closed, more or less thoroughly brutalized universe that was the peasant world of feudal Sicily, the sulfur miner made a demonic entrance: he was another sort of man, without the traditional attitude toward belongings and money, who risked his life every day, who loved to get drunk, to eat a lot, and to get into fights, who therefore threw away the little he earned by such toil, and who brutally introduced a different vision of the world. Someone, in short, who set himself to looking at the mobile and evolving aspects of life, who therefore ushered Sicilians into the heart of history. Except for Tomasi di Lampedusa, all the writers of western Sicily come directly from the world of the sulfur mines.

Marcelle Padovani. Would you say, then, that the writer is a wizard who possesses the keys if not to the total comprehension of real problems, at least to the partial approach to them?

* * *

LEONARDO SCIASCIA. The writer represents truth, true literature distinguishing itself from false only by the innate truthfulness it exhales. Let it be added, however, that this does not make the writer a philosopher or historian, but only someone who, through intuition, senses the truth. For my part, I discover in literature what I am unable to discover in the most sophisticated among the analysts who venture exhaustive interpretations and solutions for all problems. Yes, history lies, and its falsehoods envelop all the theories born of history in the same dust. Speaking of history, Paul Valéry once said what amounts to this: "I saw a letter written by the English General Shrapnel five days after the Battle of Waterloo; he declares that it was precisely the new shells invented by him that won this battle." Now, *shrapnel* is a word we never became accustomed to hearing until after the First World War. "Shrapnels" is what they called those shells that exploded at a certain height, sending out a spray of metal shards. But no one would ever have thought of using that word in talking about the Battle of Waterloo. Valéry too seemed unaware of any connection between shrapnels and Waterloo; but his interviewer pointed out that the use of shrapnels at Waterloo had been described by Stendhal: when Fabrizio sees the muddy earth being hurled twelve and fifteen feet into the air, it is clear that this is the effect, not of musketry, but of the British General Shrapnel's artillery shells.

And so it is that we discover a historical truth, not in a history textbook, but in the pages of a novel; not in a learned analysis, but between the lines of a novelistic description. Probably, Stendhal had no idea he was producing a major revelation in his description of Waterloo, yet he managed to say what nobody before him had said. Hadn't this battle always been recounted as the story of an ill-fated delay, the story of a General Blücher arriving upon the scene instead of a Marquis de Grouchy?

* * *

MARCELLE PADOVANI. This direct relationship of the writer with truth and reality, which you present as the criterion of "accurate" writing, doesn't exclude the fact that writers can make mistakes.

LEONARDO SCIASCIA. I repeat, it is the historian's information that leads the writer astray. But one must first see with regard to what and how one goes astray. The writers I know and appreciate, be they major or minor, never fool themselves about men or society or even the historical moment. Look at Manzoni. He drew a despairing portrait of Italy, but the profound truth of *The Betrothed* still hasn't been grasped. His work is generally seen as the product of a rather tranquil and conformist Italian Catholic, whereas instead it's a troubled work, which contains an uncompromising analysis of the Italian society of the time and of its most significant components. It's a book, a work that contains all of Italy, even the Italy that would later be described by De Roberto in *The Viceroys*, by Pirandello in *The Old and the Young*, and by Vitaliano Brancati in *The Old Man with the Boots*. And even the Italy of the Red Brigades.

MARCELLE PADOVANI. Cannot the writer too be mistaken about the general sense of his own work? After all, great writers like Verga and Pirandello, no doubt out of skepticism and despair, no doubt through cultural abdication, were able to adhere to fascism at a certain point.

LEONARDO SCIASCIA. Upon the significance of his personal achievement a writer can be mistaken, yes, certainly. But the work of a true writer cannot be erroneous. Pirandello was fascistic; but his work isn't.

* * *

MARCELLE PADOVANI. The philosphers of the seventeenth century asserted that *verum index sui*—truth is evident unto itself. But is a similar axiom possible in regard to writers? Or does somebody, or some norm, determine that this writer is telling the truth and some other is not?

LEONARDO SCIASCIA. Those are things that make themselves felt, and above all that are not defined once and for all. There is a veritable rotation of writers around generations, around men of flesh and blood; world literature is a kind of firmament where one sees the eclipse of certain lights and the growing brilliance of others; there are also the moments when a given writer is useful, and those in which he no longer serves, but in which he may be of service to the interests of some living persons or of entire generations. But when this writer serves it is uniquely in the sense that he aids us to live within the truth. There were centuries when Dante wasn't read and when Caravaggio didn't exist. The same thing for Petrarch, who hardly exists today even though he may be reborn. Such is the game, the great game of literature and art.

MARCELLE PADOVANI. Do you, like Gramsci, believe that a new category of intellectuals is in the process of formation—intellectuals whom Gramsci called "organic," and who, according to him, would be capable of expressing the collective thought of groups of individuals exercising a given function in society?

LEONARDO SCIASCIA.If the concept of the "organic intellectual" means—and it has meant—that the intellectual has an "organic" relationship with a political party, then I'm the most "disorganic" or "inorganic" intellectual you could find. Anyway, those words—organic, disorganic, inorganic—greatly annoy me. They make me think of manure. Of organic fertilizer. And this analogy seems to summarize the question rather nicely: the organic intellectual is a kind of manure for the political plant. In the end I'd rather be the plant than the manure that makes it grow.

MARCELLE PADOVANI. In any case, in your books there is what we might call a supplementary commitment. They force the reader to take sides, since they're written on behalf of the oppressed, on behalf of those who thirst for justice and are willing to fight for the defining of a new law...

LEONARDO SCIASCIA. I'm sure that this commitment derives from my familial condition, which furthered the development of a class instinct in me. It also comes from the experience of fascism, which was difficult and "suffered," as they say in Italy, and which made me realize that fascism could not be achieved otherwise than against me, against my interests and against the interests of everybody like me. I believe that if I became a certain kind of writer, it was through antifascist passion. My sensitivity to fascism remains very strong, I recognize it wherever it is, even when it arrays itself in the costume of antifascism, and I remain sensitive to fascism of the eternally possible Italian species. Fascism isn't finished. Given this conviction, I feel a great desire to fight it, to take my commitment further, to be ever more energetic and intransigent, to maintain a perpetually polemical attitude toward any kind of power whatever. Among the things I blame in myself as cowardly, as acts of historic and even personal cowardice, there is my not having dared come to the defense of certain fascists when it seemed to me that they were being unjustly accused. If they had been affiliated with the Left, I would have involved myself in their case ages ago, I would have signed petitions... But alas, these are products of the Right, and so, even if I scent something wrong in the way they are being dealt with, I do not feel sufficiently motivated to look more deeply into the matter.

MARCELLE PADOVANI. A question or two on how it all started. How was it that the urge to write came to possess a Sicilian schoolteacher in the second half of the twentieth century, a schoolteacher who had therefore known fascism during his adolescence and seen Sicily gradually emerge from the darkest underdevelopment? What incited you to take pen in hand, and by what process did you reach the conclusion that you were a writer?

LEONARDO SCIASCIA. I grew up surrounded by women—my aunts, one of whom taught in the elementary school, and my mother, who rarely left the house. Homes were then the places of choice for the observation of things and people, and there I would remain with skirts all about me, I would listen in silence, and I would end up finding out everything that was happening in the village, from the first to the last piece of gossip, from the least tattle to the latest rumor: what is literature, after all, if not an immense anthology of tittle-tattle? So people came in, swapped tales, and I watched all the passions, family dramas, and other people's intimacies file under my miscroscope. It left me with an insatiable curiosity about the most minute details of life. And that is how I became a writer: it's an activity that's rendered infinitely easier when you find yourself in the midst of women.

For many years I didn't think of making a profession out of it, even though I loved to write and had written a lot right away. I got my image of the writer in Caltanisetta, in 1937–1938, for Brancati was teaching in the school I attended. Every week he published a "Letter from Caltanisetta" in *Omnibus* magazine, in which, with that irony and sense of the quotidian that I so admired, he discussed things I knew all about. That's when the idea occurred to me that I, too, could be a writer, that I could be like Brancati—an idea, however, that was grafted onto a genuine, preexisting mania for writing: I was already writing everywhere, even on chunks of wood, putting down everything that popped into my head. A mannered graphomaniac during the thirties in Caltanisetta, that's what I was . . .

In my house there always breathed a boundless respect for things having to do with writing—a respect and fear typical of the peasant world. For the peasant, is not writing necessarily fraud, imposture, and falsification? I like to recall a riddle that goes:

> Bianca campagna,
> nera semenza,
> l'uomo che la fa
> sempre la pensa.

The "white countryside" is the sheet of paper, the "black seeds" are the written words, the "man who sows" is the person who's writing and who must remain ever vigilant, all the while thinking of what he is doing, of the power he holds in his hands. It's a riddle from my region, and the real message it contains is this: who must always think of writing if it is not the peasant who knows neither how to read nor to write and who is forever at the mercy of the man who does know? Things have always been *recounted* to the peasant, he never apprised himself of them on his own initiative, and that is why, when in 1974 the electoral campaign began for the referendum on divorce, and Sicilian women were told that if the right to divorce were approved their husbands would abandon them, some believed that talk. How can you expect peasants not to be mistrustful of what is told to them or what exists in writing?

From writing-as-deceit such as it was in the eyes of the peasant and such as it had been for me, I moved ahead to the perception of writing-as-truth, and I convinced myself that if truth necessarily has several facets, the only possible form of truth is that of art. The writer, I repeat, discloses the truth by deciphering reality and shedding light upon the incomprehensions that denature it; but in unveiling certain aspects of the real he may at the same time make things more obscure, for among the properties of writing is that of conveying certain obscurities. Take the case of Raymond Roussel, who died in Palermo. In my attempt to introduce some order into the documents about him, in seeking among them for a thread and a logic, I fear I rendered things not clearer but more obscure. There is, however, a difference between this obscurity and that of ignorance: it is no longer the obscurity of the unexpressed, of the shapeless, but the obscurity of the expressed and formulated. This is why I often employ the "discourse" of the detective story, a form of narrative aimed toward the truth of the facts and the indictment of the culprit, even if the culprit can't always be found. These days I've begun to think that only one thing would please me. Do you remember what Malraux said about Faulkner? That he had brought about the "intrusion of Greek tragedy into the detective story." I'd so much like to have it said of me that I introduced Pirandellian drama into the detective story!

Of me as an individual—an individual who, incidentally, wrote books—I'd like people to say, "He was contradictory and self-contradictory," as a way of saying that I was alive in the midst of so many "dead souls," so many people who weren't contradictory and who never contradicted themselves.

V. Concerning Power—Communist Power Especially

MARCELLE PADOVANI. You have had, and perhaps still do, a strange relationship with the Italian Communist Party. You have sometimes said that it is the party you feel the closest to, but one gets the impression that you've passed from critical friendship to a certain violence in its regard. In *Equal Danger* you have a Christian Democrat say: "My party, which has misgoverned for thirty years, had the hunch that it might misgovern better together with the international revolutionary party." And in *Candido* you seem to wish to settle accounts once and for all. In that book the PCI appears ignorant, bogged down in Stalinism, looking in anything but a revolutionary direction, timorous, and full of bureaucrats without intelligence and without heart.

But to confront the problem in more global terms, and as you examine the place that the PCI occupies in Italian society, do you not feel that this party's position has been nearly reversed in the space of a two-year period? In 1976 the PCI collects 34.5% of the vote after having allowed ten per cent of the room on its lists for non-communists, Catholics, economists, intellectuals, independents. In 1975 you yourself were one of these "independents on the PCI ticket" elected to the Palermo city council.

Well, it does indeed seem that those strata that had moved toward the PCI have tended, beginning in 1978, to move away from it, the result being that this party, over and above its internal problems and its relationship with its own base, is at present in the midst of a rather severe crisis in its relations with the non-communists, and that amongst the latter intolerance is tending to prevail over informed criticism. What happened to the strategy and practice of the PCI between 1976 and 1978 that can explain this rift, given that the "historic compromise," with which even the Left reproaches it so often, dates back to 1973, and that instead of discouraging the electorate, spurred the electorate to vote en masse for the PCI in 1976?

LEONARDO SCIASCIA. The votes that the PCI obtained in 1976—the *additional* votes—are certainly going to recede. And the recession may perhaps go beyond that. Undoubtedly, that portion of the bourgeoisie that voted for the PCI as the "party of order" will continue to give it support; but I doubt whether the old communist base, especially in the South, will do the same. The extra votes it obtained in 1976 were in my judgment a kind of fatality, a nemesis for the PCI. Vespasian said that money has no odor. But votes do; and sometimes they even have a bad odor. The support of the Italian "man of order" represents gifts it were wise to be wary of. *Timeo Danaos et dona ferentes*. . . .

I believe that a conversation on communism in general is indispensable. Let's turn to the map of communist states. Since the leadership and the myth of the Soviet Union have crumbled, since Stalinism has been desacralized by Khruschev, the tension has shifted (so to speak) from the USSR to the whole of the communist world. The first simple conclusion to be drawn from this is that the heat is on everyone for no one has achieved veritable socialism, nor does anyone possess even in embryonic form that which is necessary to its achievement. So it seems to me completely legitimate that the countries which aren't yet communist ask themselves how likely it is that socialism, which they do not see achieved or at the budding stage anywhere else, will be realized on their own soil; and that the people who ask themselves this question most often are the Italians, they who have a communist party that is strong and not far from power. In recent years this question has become more urgent, given the formidable ambiguity that the Italian, French, and Spanish communist parties continue to manifest with regard to the Soviet Union and other communist countries. On the one hand, they put forward judgments and propositions that ought to lead to a break; on the other hand, they declare that their ties with the communist parties of the Eastern European nations are still strong, nay, indissoluble. There's an interesting book on European communism by Bettiza, who concludes with two statements by Berlinguer, made within a short span of time and yet in absolute contradiction with one another. I confess that I did not immediately credit these citations, I wanted to verify them; and I found that Bettiza had not made them up. There, I said to myself, there are excellent reasons for the voter also to be mistrustful and begin to back off.

Then, if we continue to examine this map of the communist countries, we discover something similar to the Christian world after the advent of Protestantism. The states that called themselves Christian were worst enemies among one another, and it wasn't at all unusual for a Christian state to form an alliance with, for example, the Turks. The communist states are in the same situation: China today may objectively consider itself an ally of the United States, while in their turn the Americans feel themselves the allies both of China and of the USSR. The two greatest communist countries thus pursue policies that are not fundamentally different from those the Christian states once pursued, and whose principle is this: the enemy of my enemy is my friend.

Rivarol used to say that there are two absolutely inseparable truths in the world: the first is that sovereignty resides in the people; the second, that the people are never to exercise it. A large part of humanity believed that with communism these two truths became dissociable. But the domestic and foreign policies of the communist countries have taught us that the two truths are not separate and are not going to separate.

MARCELLE PADOVANI. May it not be maintained, first of all, that these communist countries have undergone different, sometimes contradictory evolutions; and, secondly, that there have been different communist parties in the West?

LEONARDO SCIASCIA. There are evolutions; even more so there are involutions. The evolutions consist above all in the attempt to adapt to the Western model, and to transform initially poor societies into consumer societies. But that is not what one expected from Marxist parties. From them one expected what Marx calls "the new man." And that's exactly where they have failed.

MARCELLE PADOVANI. Inside the communist countries, however, you have the courageous positions taken by for example Polish and Czech dissidents, those who criticize their respective regimes not in order to move towards the Western model, but rather in the name of an authentic Marxism...

LEONARDO SCIASCIA. I respect their positions, but I believe that the idea of an "authentic Marxism" amounts to a utopia within a utopia, a dream, an illusion. All that I know of communism, everything in communism that disappoints me and embitters me, does not incline me to be anticommunist, precisely because I think of the people who still believe in it. The Eastern dissidents who still profess to be socialists base their confidence in the future on the idea that those regimes may one day be able to find sufficient resources within themselves to take the path of socialism, and on the other idea that in a socialist country there is something which on the intellectual level is attractive and in a certain sense aristocratic and esthetically appealing: I mean poverty. I feel a bit the same way. The only socialist country that I have had the occasion to come to know is Yugoslavia. The first time I set foot on Yugoslav soil, crossing the border from an Italy overflowing with advertising posters, automobiles, noise, and things to eat, I felt almost happy. The people in that part of the world had occasion to concern themselves with so many things that we no longer pay attention to. It was clear that feelings, real beauty, the things of life mattered more to them than they did to us. Even later on I remained greatly attached to Yugoslavia; I would feel good there and I would feel my old self. Then, in recent years, I've seen Yugoslavia change too; and by now I can see no difference between Ljubljana and Gorizia. Consequently Yugoslavia seems less seductive, even though I notice that the Yugoslavs seem happier today than before. I strongly doubt whether the communist party's massive following would now accept to share poverty among themselves, their only wish at present being to have consumer goods distributed to them. If they demand justice, it is in the distribution of riches, not of poverty.

At this point in the argument I should say that although I lack any firsthand knowledge of the USSR—which I've approached only through books, or through contacts with writers—I believe that, all things considered, it still remains the country with the most socialism, or perhaps the most Christianity. It strikes me that a man like Solzhenitsyn, even in his dissidence, in the expression of his opinions, which can appear medieval, is the involuntary product of that socialism or that Christianity. As for the dissidents in Poland and Czechoslovakia, they are like those heretics who searched for true Christianity and never found it. But at least Christianity offers the individual the possibility of being Christian, even to the point of saintliness. Whereas a socialist state offers no possibility of being socialist: there everybody's a socialist, or else nobody is. But what is new nowadays is that we can talk about socialism in the way that at the close of the last century they talked about liberalism in Europe—a liberalism which was a live subject precisely because it was dead.

I'd like to be clearly understood here. In each of us, even those who believe they have been far removed from it, the solicitation of the socialist idea yet endures and shall endure, like the solicitation of Christianity and for the same reason. Did not Benedetto Croce say that "We cannot not be Christians" (even if one's rejoinder must be that at the time the world was hardly Christian)? Today we can say that "We cannot not be socialists," even as we observe socialism register, on the level of human communities, failures graver still than those of Christianity.

MARCELLE PADOVANI. And if, resuming the argument, one were to ask whether these countries called "communist" have anything to do with "socialism"?

LEONARDO SCIASCIA. It's the "if" connected with Cleopatra's nose, as Pascal said. If we consider that an additional three millimeters of nose in Cleopatra's profile might have made all the difference in the history of the Mediterranean basin and of the world . . . but then we tumble into a romance which will make history appear more and more absurd to us and more and more of a soap opera. The one advantage I'd see in it is that it would perhaps free us from this sickness of believing in history as providence and as finality. In this sense, yes, we might start again to look at history the way Pascal did, and the way Voltaire did too, despite the abyss which separated the two men.

MARCELLE PADOVANI. And in your opinion this excludes the possibility of criticizing (and, eventually, amending) those societies in the name of Marxism?

LEONARDO SCIASCIA. We judge those countries upon their practices and in the light of the theory that guides them. It is possible that they have attained a degree or a mode of socialism that theory did not foresee. But in that case you must have the courage to say that the theory did not serve, that it is not serving, that everywhere they are proceeding with their eyes closed, or at any rate according to the purest pragmatism.

MARCELLE PADOVANI. Is that also your view regarding the Third World countries where Marxism is still the only theory, and the only technique, for the liberation of peoples?

LEONARDO SCIASCIA. I think that the Third World countries are still the seat of imperialism, and that, paradoxically, Marxism reaches them as one of the incarnations of imperialism and is espoused, by their developing ruling classes, as an instrument of power. It seems to me, in short, that these countries are going through a phase comparable to what the Risorgimento was for Southern Italy.

MARCELLE PADOVANI. And the communist parties of the West—have they not undergone different evolutions and have they not worked out an elaboration specific to each of them, each time within a particular context?

LEONARDO SCIASCIA. From the standpoint of theory, yes, I would maintain that they are on the same level. From the standpoint of practice, it is quite true that each has its particularity. But all of them are in an impasse. As of the moment when the USSR ceased to be a model or a myth, when Stalinism was laid bare and revealed itself to be a frightful variety of fascism, these parties have lost their sense of direction.

We may take the case of the Italian Communist Party. I realize that its politics may appear coherent and oriented straight ahead. When Togliatti, the party's secretary general, returns to Italy in 1944 when the country is still cut in two, he accepts the principle of the monarchy, participates in the government, pleads for peace between Italians, grants amnesty to the fascists, votes for Article 7 of the Constitution which confirms the Concordat; then, just when he could have lost his good sense (after his attempted assassination in 1948), gives proof of his political ability—the masses who are PCI militants or vote for it remain authorized in their belief that behind this reassuring physiognomy, the leader of the party is hiding his revolutionary's "mental reserve." In fine, that even if power is not taken by revolutionary methods, revolution, one day or another, will be accomplished. Because there is the USSR, because there is Stalin; because together they are the guarantee that the end the communists are pursuing remains worldwide revolution, the guarantee that the communist party remains a revolutionary party. And when Kruschev comes onto the stage with his string of revelations, the spell is broken. But the masses are still not completely overpowered by events; they consider that, everything taken into account, this too must be part of the reassuring make-believe that communism is playing opposite the worldwide bourgeoisie—part, that is, of its "mental reserve."

Until 1976. I believe that up until that point, not only the communist base but also the first-time PCI voters knew that they were supporting a still Stalinist party, a party therefore capable, once it headed the government, of being tough and of running Italy with an iron hand. A *revolutionary* party for the communist militants; for the petty bourgeois and the middle-class voting communist for the first time, a party standing for *order*. Now, it was precisely during those two years that the PCI clearly revealed itself to its base as a non-revolutionary party or as one that had ceased to be revolutionary, a party without either the strength or the means to change Italy in a revolutionary sense. Well, as the great communist Concetto Marchesi once said, the moment a revolutionary party stops being revolutionary, it ceases to be *anything at all*.

MARCELLE PADOVANI. In your opinion, what should have been the attitude of a truly revolutionary party during these crucial last two years in Italy, taking into account the economic crisis and the rampant terrorism?

LEONARDO SCIASCIA. I shall resume my argument. The mistrust of the communist base—which will not necessarily lead to its abandoning the PCI but perhaps simply to its resigning itself—finds a curious echo in the mistrust of that portion of the bourgeoisie which voted communist in 1976. The crucial moment in this mistrust was, in my opinion, the Moro affair. The PCI at the time had managed to push the Christian Democrats, notoriously devoid of any sense of state, into assuming an attitude of intransigent defense of the values of that same state. One could therefore think that the PCI had issued, via the Christian Democrats, a reassuring message, a message in defense of order. But behind the reassuring message people discerned a much more troubling one: that the Christian Democrats were losing the one particularity they had ever possessed, by which I mean their Christianity; that during the Moro affair people were beholding a different DC, one that no longer corresponded to the expectations of the majority of the Italians who had voted for it; that, yes, the PCI was a party that represented order, but an order obtained through the intermediary of the DC... a denatured order. And the Italians were troubled by this.

MARCELLE PADOVANI. That didn't stop them, did it, from giving the Christian Democrats a higher percentage of votes—four percent more—in the municipal elections of May 1978, a few days after the discovery of Aldo Moro's corpse.

LEONARDO SCIASCIA. They voted Christian Democrat to help that party regain its identity. In effect, the order the communists were able to dictate was still the old order of the old Italian state, which, to quote Pietro Nenni, is weak with the strong and strong with the weak. The weak one, in this case, was Aldo Moro, and it was only with him that the state, defended by the communists, was able to show itself strong and give itself Prussian airs. The strong were the men of the Red Brigades, and with them the state showed itself to be particularly weak and ineffectual. In the confrontation with the Red Brigades, the communists' power, their strength, their organization served for nothing at all unless it was to allow Aldo Moro to be killed.

MARCELLE PADOVANI. A good many intellectuals didn't wait for the Moro affair to distance themselves from the PCI, among them the ones who had orchestrated support for it in 1976. You yourself gave a signal of disaffection in January 1977 when you presented your resignation from the Palermo city council to which you had been elected "on the PCI ticket" in June of 1975.

LEONARDO SCIASCIA. Let's say that the majority of the intellectuals, in betting on the PCI, were putting their money on the horse they thought would win. But so far I see no great turning away from that party; the intellectuals, from what I can make out, while in private they are critical of the PCI and even sharply critical, continue in public to express a certain reverence for it. If distrust there be on their part, it remains of a very prudent sort.

My own personal case is very much bound up with the local Sicilian situation. I joined the Palermo PCI ticket as a noncommunist in the municipal elections of 1975. My "entry" had been solicited by local leaders and presented as an event that was sure to have consequences at the local level. And indeed there were consequences, and prompt ones: incited by the example of the PCI to renew its candidates, the Christian Democrats were obliged to tidy up its lists by excluding the more compromised personalities (like, for example, the famous Ciancimino, reputedly close to the Mafia and who had been the Christian Democrat mayor of Palermo) and by including a certain number of intellectuals of its own. Naturally the DC had placed these intellectuals in slots where they had no chance of being elected; they served only as window-dressing. While those who appeared on the PCI ticket were all elected. The PCI increased by four the number of seats it had won in previous municipal elections, getting a total of fifteen out of eighty. We constituted, so to speak, an "absolute minority," but only on condition we conducted a determined and courageous opposition which could make an impact on the national level and demonstrate that we were the antithesis of everything the Christian Democrats could produce in the way of administration.

But when the new city council set about business, the Communist Party decided to seek a meeting of minds with the Christian Democrats—without it ever being clear what that might imply—instead of chosing to stay within a coherent opposition. Now, at the time, Palermo was beset by extremely serious problems. In certain neighorhoods there was no water, entire groups of apartment buildings were connected to no sewer system, had no paved streets, and the restoration or rehabilitation of the city's "historic" center was turning out to be difficult: for example, certain blocks of dwellings still contained unexploded mines and bombs dropped in the course of the 1943 Allied air raids. During the eighteen months I spent on the city council, the water supply never came up for discussion even once. The question of sanitation was addressed in, so it seemed to me, an incomprehensible manner (upon this subject a discussion about Sakharov once arose . . .) and only later and in an altogether private way was I made acquainted with the concrete terms of the problem, thanks to the goodwill of a socialist assessor, who explained to me how desirable it was that the improvements be contracted out to different construction companies in accordance with the method of public bidding, and that bids be solicited from all the companies located outside Palermo as well as inside. The PCI, however, in accord with the Christian Democrats, proposed that bids be sought only from Palermo enterprises under the pretext that they were the only verifiable ones; to me that seemed the surest way to open the door to every conceivable manipulation.

Considering that my presence on the city council was inopportune and to no purpose, and that a clash between myself and the party that had got me elected was growing more and more likely, I thought it normal that I present my resignation. I wanted to leave without slamming the door, but to do so was not possible.

MARCELLE PADOVANI. At the time you explained your resignation as a response to the inefficiency of Palermo's city council, you alluded to how much time was wasted during meetings, you mentioned the fact that although the council members were convoked at nine in the evening, business was not addressed until around eleven o'clock or midnight.

LEONARDO SCIASCIA. Punctuality is more than just a problem of form: it is a kind of respect for oneself, for institutions and for the electorate. And it also, and above all, indicates the will to get things done. A city council that meets at ten o'clock and doesn't get down to work until midnight can do nothing else but nod its distracted, weary assent to whatever is put before it. And this is precisely what is wanted: approval, not discussion and criticism.

Those who had voted for me took the announcement of my resignation as an alarm signal, and rightly so. My candidacy occurred as a local event, and it was concluded on the local level with criticisms that had a local significance. Consequently without a disagreement between the PCI and myself. The disagreement came later.

MARCELLE PADOVANI. With the "cowardice" episode. The trial of the Red Brigades in Turin was then running up against all sorts of difficulties, not the least of which was the formation of a popular jury: as each of their names came up, the jurors advanced reasons of health (they one by one fell prey to a "depressive syndrome") as they declined the task of judging the *brigatisti*. Actually it was a question of fear, the terrorists not having hesitated to assassinate their judges. You then stepped in and declared that you, too, were unable to identify with this "state in the throes of decomposition" and that, were it not for the "duty not to be afraid," you also would have refused to serve on the jury. The writer Italo Calvino had taken a different position, declaring that "we are all the state"; you had the approval of the philosopher Norberto Bobbio, while Giorgio Amendola, one of the "historic leaders" of the PCI, evoked the "cowardice of the intellectuals," maintaining that "civic courage has never been a very widespread quality within the broad spheres of Italian culture." Why did you feel it incumbent upon you to declare your solidarity with the "excused" jurors in Turin, and how do you feel today about this onetime polemic?

LEONARDO SCIASCIA. I intervened because of an article by Italo Calvino, who had expressed his discomfort and his despair before the attitude of Eugenio Montale, who had called "understandable" the refusal of the sixteen citizens of Turin to serve on the jury. At that point I felt the need to join the debate: I too understood the sixteen citizens, just as I understood Montale, and I did indeed add that had it not been for the duty not to be afraid—a duty I felt toward myself and not toward the state—I too would have declined the burdensome honor of serving on the jury. What guarantees, I asked, did this state offer, not only to insure the protection of the citizens who assume the risk of serving on juries, but to promote the safeguarding of rights, the application of the law, and the triumph of justice? What guarantees against theft, against the abuse of power, against injustice? None. The reigning impunity for all crimes committed against the collectivity and against public property was worthy of a regime of the South American type. Not a single one of the major scandals that had occurred over the last thirty years had ever been elucidated, not one of those responsible had been punished; reigning in the state's highest office was the very controversial Giovanni Leone, who would be forced to tender his resignation on June 15, 1978; in every city and in every village it was possible to compile an interminable list of embezzlements, of cases of misappropriation and other abuses that remained unpunished; and the citizens who performed their duties, first of all as simple taxpayers, regularly saw themselves first led around by the nose and then laughed at, not only because others shirked their fiscal obligations, but also because the laws that the Republic itself enacted were unjust. Had not the "fiscal pardon" just restored to innocence all those who had cheated the tax authorities, which represented a bonus for not respecting the law, an encouragement to be a bad citizen rather than a good one?

Then I asked that we look at the functioning of the public services, where the only thing to see is their inadaptation to the modern world and their growing inefficiency: the school which had essentially ceased to exist, the postal service, the railroads, the airlines, all in chaos along with the hospitals. The liberal professions, and the physicians especially, become the principal pillar of corruption in the country. The upper echelons of the bureaucracy decimated by absurd laws like those concerning "early retirement," which enables big wheels to pocket remarkable severance packages before going and getting themselves rehired at a better salary in another branch of the administration, nay, even in the same one. Things and events which were—and which continue to be—almost beyond belief.

And it's in this country, which lives under such conditions, that Amendola esteems it "cowardly" to say that this state doesn't deserve to be defended! Incredible! For him the state must be a kind of mythical and metaphysical entity, superior to anything like the rendering of services. For me, the state is nothing but a well-coordinated ensemble of services. And when these services are deficient or altogether absent, it's necessary either to fix them or to create new ones. Otherwise all you are defending is corruption and inefficiency under the pretext of defending the state.

MARCELLE PADOVANI. I don't know what Amendola's underlying thinking was when he made his remark about "cowardice." But is it not hypothetically possible that he didn't mean to defend the state as unfeeling and abstract monster, or the state as ensemble of services raised to the level of myth, but simply the state founded on the Constitution, and democracy, which, in his opinion, the terrorists were endangering?

LEONARDO SCIASCIA. I don't think there was any underlying thought behind Amendola's accusation. There was simply the desire for an authoritarian state—and to avoid offending him I'll call it a Stalinist rather than a fascist state—, and a visceral aversion to nonconformist writers. As for the Constitution and democracy: does the Constitution still exist? An expert, a jurist named Mario d'Antonio, has written a very interesting book, *The Paper Constitution*, that is to say, the Constitution which henceforth exists on paper only and not in the country's reality.

MARCELLE PADOVANI. The fact that despite the threats, despite the assassinations, the Red Brigades trial was able to take place—doesn't that represent, after all, a positive event?

LEONARDO SCIASCIA. It is something positive above all for the citizens who had the courage to serve as judges or jurors. Those—if we set the number of persons who served against the number who refused—represent five percent of the Italian population. That means that ninety-five percent of Italian citizens feel, as I do, that the state being what it now is, they have no duty to defend it. I am merely quoting the figures and commenting on them; I'm not exhorting anyone to abandon the state; I'm simply pointing out that in their virtual unanimity Italians refuse to identify themselves with it.

And so, you see, I believe that on balance it would have been preferable that this trial not take place. What did we witness for months and months? The performance staged by the Red Brigades. It was the terrorists, in effect, who called the tune, not the judges; it was the terrorists who made a mockery of the judicial system, and not the reverse. I read the coverage of the trial by foreign journalists: more so than their Italian colleagues, they were appalled to see justice flouted every day in front of their eyes; appalled by the incredible confusion, the continuous humiliation of the judges, the unbounded arrogance of the terrorists. It was a hallucinatory spectacle. I don't think that anything decent came out of that trial.

MARCELLE PADOVANI. If the trial had not taken place, if the Red Brigades had succeeded in paralyzing the justice system, would the state have presented a better picture of itself? Wouldn't there have been people denouncing "this state's inability to try criminals"?

LEONARDO SCIASCIA. But the Italian state had already shown itself incapable of putting plenty of other criminals on trial; one trial more or less wouldn't have made a whole lot of difference ... What I mean to say is that no end of trials should have taken place over the past thirty years and never did. The one against the Red Brigades should have been deferred until the moment when it might have been possible to put on a less miserable performance.

MARCELLE PADOVANI. In the course of that lengthy debate, many stepped in to explain that the state was something other than, and more than, an assortment of organs of repression or an accumulation of bureaucracies. That the state was the Constitution, considered one of the most democratic in the world. That it was also the conquests of the workers' movement, such as the achieving of a voice in the way work is organized, in company investments, in employment policies—; that it was also the legislative and contractual limits imposed on the owners' absolute power. That it was, finally, the growth of the political representation of the workers themselves in the various elected assemblies as well as on the level of neighborhoods, municipalities, regions, etc.

LEONARDO SCIASCIA. The state is the Constitution when it does truly embody it. Nowadays, it is nothing but an empty container.

MARCELLE PADOVANI. But let's get back to the Italian Communist Party, which was the state's main champion during the Moro affair, thereby incurring your criticisms. Why were you to such a point surprised by the PCI's attitude? What had been the reasons for your rapprochement with this party? I recall that when I came to see you in Palermo in 1975, you explained the reasons for your presence on the communist slate: you spoke of this party as a "symbol of cleanliness," you spoke of it as a "bearer of culture." I even had occasion to read your statement in the 1976 party almanac, where you specified the reasons for the stand you had taken: "The PCI is different," you wrote, "from the image it gave of itself at a particular historic moment; different above all from the image that its adversaries stubbornly attribute to it." Then you added: "All the truth as regards socialism has been said: against it there is yet being waged a long, tedious, unbearable, and above all pointless war. Today we find ourselves on the PCI slate, and it is in order to make our small contribution to the abreviating of this long and stupid war . . ." Why today do you no longer agree with the things you said at an earlier time?

LEONARDO SCIASCIA. In the constat that may be drawn up of the present-day ruin of Italy, it is certain that the greatest responsibilities belong to the Christian Democrats. But since for thirty years we have, at least formally, enjoyed a perfectly democratic system, we cannot but attribute a sizable share of responsibility to the opposition as well. I would say that the opposition constitutes the most delicate part in the workings of the democratic apparatus; and I simply do not understand this tendency of the Italian Communist Party to rid itself of the task of opposition in the name of God knows what *unity of all the constitutional forces in the face of dangers threatening the economy and democracy*—the unity, that is, of all the forces that accept the Constitution and the democratic method: and what a lot of them there are! This attitude would be understandable if it were only tactical and intended to win the PCI recognition as the constitutional and democratic party. But the moment the tactic becomes a strategy, it ceases to be understandable. For, after all, if every single democratic party ends up joining the government, who will take on the task of the opposition? The fascists? Let's be frank: is it normal, is it sane, is it just that the most essential and delicate part of the democratic apparatus should be entrusted to a nondemocratic party—worse still, to an openly fascist one?

But my own relationship with the PCI has been extremely complex, almost as complex as the one I've entertained with Sicily. A love-hate relationship, to simplify. In 1974–1975 I approached the party, or, to be more exact, the PCI approached me; in the light of this coming together it appeared to me different. Human relations, personal contacts mean a great deal to me: certain younger PCI functionaries gave me the impression that the party had changed, or that it was on the point of doing so.

My ensuing experience on the city council was a complete disappointment. The party wasn't changing. In a certain sense, it was even getting worse. Hence I had made an error in judgment; but it was also a liberating experience. For the PCI I no longer have any form of respect. I still like the people who are in it, but I consider this party the most superannuated there is: even more ancient than the liberal party.

MARCELLE PADOVANI. France has had a "good opposition" for over thirty years. Its communist party is important—from 21 to 22 percent of the vote—and it has always incarnated, sometimes with violence, the toughest of oppositions. More, in 1978 it preferred to throw away its chances of participating in the government within the framework of the "Union of the Left" rather than abandon its role as the opposition, and have inevitably to "dirty its hands" in the direct management of the economic crisis. What purpose does this communist party serve, the French pundits are always asking, since the parliamentary opposition enjoys very few rights under the system that has arisen under the Fifth Republic, and the labor union opposition, at grips with a body of employers particularly attached to the defense of their prerogatives, is unable to impose the right to negotiate. It seems that the cult of the opposition—once characteristic of the Right before becoming the favorite theme of certain Italian leftists and the French New Philosophers—has so far produced two results: it has insured that the government of the European states remains in the hands of a conservative majority, and that the opposition (with the communists) never accedes to power. Would you agree?

LEONARDO SCIASCIA. In France the majority does grab all the room for itself. But in Italy the opposition may have more space, the majority-versus-opposition game being nearer to the way the thing is played in England. In France the powers of the president are considerable; in France they got a left-wing government in 1936, and it failed. You see, I believe the Left is destined to be the perfect opposition through its very long-standing tradition of protest, and also for more recent reasons (I have in mind the Yalta agreements, designed, among other things, to prevent the communist Left from coming to power). So if the Left is destined to be the opposition, let it at least do a good job of it!

To return to the Italian communists, I feel that the PCI chose to be a mirror, the Christian Democrats' mirror, or that it literally contemplated itself in the Christian Democrats as if in a mirror, moreover mistaking for left what was actually right, and right for left. I am not saying that it did not play an oppositional role at all; it did play one, but one that was marginal, incomplete and incompetent. Does that ask to explained? Reforms were attempted in Italy. Now, by what does one recognize the contribution of an opposition if not by the fact that is able to call for reforms, but able also to contribute to the modifying of their contents. On this score, alas, it seems that the communist opposition—whose intelligence and competence was recognized by everyone, even by its adversaries—was not forthcoming. Thus there are two hypotheses that can be formulated: either the PCI was not capable of constituting a good opposition, and the Italians attributed to it qualities it did not have; or it played the game of "well, well, it might be worse" with "the government that works least works best." I take the example of land reform in Sicily, a reform that did not benefit from any contribution of intelligence or competence. Through it, the government was content to proceed to expropriations, offering generous indemnities to the owners, and land was distributed in tiny plots to the peasants, who have been forced little by little to abandon them, for they were given no leg-up by the banks, or else did not possess adequate tools to work them. Another example: the industrialization of Sicily: the cost involved, let's say, in maintaining the sulfur mines in operation and then shutting them down. On the national level there's much worse: you have only to look at what Montedison has become, along with all the rest of nationalized industry, which is by now no more than a knot of clienteles organized with the aim of squandering public money. What did the opposition do, what did the Communist Party do, to avoid this degradation?

I believe that in order to understand the PCI today, one must constantly refer oneself to that "looking-glass" relationship with the Christian Democrats. The DC, too, has watched itself living in the PCI. The result? It is a fine one: these two parties have indissolubly linked their forces, nay, their destinies. On the electoral level, it is striking: PCI and DC swap percentages back and forth; a big DC without a big PCI is inconceivable, as is the contrary. It's a situation that dates from 1948. In later years, factors that I would call sociological have come into play, factors that have to do with modifications in life-style, in economic level, in behavior. Today's left-winger no longer lives like the romantic man of the Left of bygone days who was so utterly different from the right-winger no one could mistake one for the other. An example of this old-fashioned, nearly extinct man of the Left? Girolamo Li Causi, one of the PCI's historic figures and who indeed founded the party in Sicily. I think Li Causi was the only member of parliament who refused to become the proprietor of a house. Today, the new men of the Left lead the same lives as the men of the Center and the Right: the same houses, the same hobbies, the same social circles. What's taken place is the process that Pier Paolo Pasolini called "homologation." Consequently I believe that we can give an equally sociological explanation for the PCI-sponsored "historic compromise." Instead of viewing it only as a political response to the events in Chile, to the fear of right-wing reaction, to despair of ever being able to gain control of the state either by way of ballot box or revolution, we might also explain it as the result of a change in our national mores.

Obviously all this does not prevent the PCI from having represented and from continuing to represent that which is the best part of the nation, that is to say, the people who work, the honest and serious people. But these people are about to be betrayed by a party in the midst of mutation. At the point where we are now, either the PCI breaks absolutely and cleanly with the Soviet Union and becomes a vaguely Marxist and absolutely not Leninist party, but rather of the social-democratic type, animated by various inner currents; or the Christian Democrats and the center manage to thrust it back into the opposition, and then the PCI will go back to its former rigid Leninist self, becoming fellow traveler to the Red Brigades.

MARCELLE PADOVANI. And you, what do you hope for?

LEONARDO SCIASCIA. That it becomes a social-democratic party.

MARCELLE PADOVANI. And yet it seems to me that you have at various times expressed a kind of nostalgia for Stalinism, or rather for the Stalinist epoch, when the masses had the feeling of belonging to a revolutionary party; when the PCI was at the heights of its *doppiezza*, thinking one thing and saying another—indulging in the luxury of officially preaching in favor of parliamentary democracy while preserving a hidden intention, the violent conquest of power. Do you regret the passing of Stalinism, and from what point of view?

LEONARDO SCIASCIA. No, I do not mourn the myth of Stalin in itself, nor that of the USSR in its historic reality, in its concrete truth; but rather as a myth for the masses who had no direct experience of the country or of the man. The myth of the USSR and Stalin served to secure the monolithic character and the religious firmness of the PCI. The people of that era didn't expect the party to offer them jobs or favors or preferential treatment when contracts were up for bidding. From it they expected revolution, total change, the entering into a new way of being and thinking. Let's say that personally I don't regret the passing of Stalinism, but that, after Stalin and without Stalin, I think the PCI ought to have lived as Dostoevsky invited us to live after the death of God: "Stalin does not exist, and therefore nothing is permitted." Instead the axiom it chose was "Stalin is no more, therefore everything is permitted."

I think also of all the energy the PCI spent upon making the United States unpopular in Italy, and the Vietnamese cause popular... If they had devoted that energy to sending to prison all those who deserved to go there, all the corrupt and dishonest ones, and to seeing to it that competent, serious people were put in charge of public affairs, then in my opinion they would have better acquitted themselves of their duties and better served their electorate.

MARCELLE PADOVANI. There are those who insist that the PCI, starting from the moment it defined the "historic compromise," and above all when it came out as an intransigent defender of the state during the Moro affair, has chosen to give the country's interests a priority over its own interests as a party, deliberately accepting a loss of votes (nine percentage points in the municipal elections of May 14, 1978) in order to save a democracy that it considered to be in peril.

LEONARDO SCIASCIA. I believe the communists took the road toward inevitable suicide. Their behavior during the Moro affair was part of that suicidal syndrome, for it is true and profound madness that a party take upon itself sins that are not its own, and proclaim itself guardian to Christian Democracy, a role that nobody had asked it to assume. In the same way, when Luciano Lama, a communist, hies himself to the University of Rome and harangues the students with the aim of restoring order among them, I would submit that he is taking upon himself a sacrifice that nobody has asked for. And then, of course, my idea of the Left is, let's say, of something vital. The Left is life. And yet during the Moro affair it aligned itself with death. The communist Left, at any rate. The socialists defended another line.

MARCELLE PADOVANI. Beyond what one may hold to be an "error" on the part of the PCI, which is your position, don't you think that something is beginning to emerge in Europe, a kind of repugnance at seeing the communists participating in government? Doesn't it seem as if just about everywhere a limit has been reached beyond which it is no longer tolerable, for certain forces, that the working class movement continue to advance within institutions and to bring all its weight to bear upon economic and political decisions? Aren't the forces of the Right picking up steam just about everywhere?

LEONARDO SCIASCIA. Yes, the Right has the advantage again. Not because it has identified the strength of the communist parties, but their weakness. What happened in Portugal, in my opinion, marked the turnaround. It was established there that communist parties can lose at the very moment they believe they are winning. I fear that this outcome is going to be reproduced often enough to become a constant in European history over the next ten years. The second country to undergo this experience may well be Italy, where the PCI entered into the most critical of phases at the very moment everyone was convinced that it was about to win.

MARCELLE PADOVANI. However, the Western communist parties have a totally divergent vision on such formidable problems as the building of a united Europe, NATO, the administration of austerity. The PCI, for example, has concerned itself more with these problems than the French or Spanish communist parties.

LEONARDO SCIASCIA. I don't think the communist parties are so very different from one another. Their structures are identical, as are their mentalities. The differences are solely verbal. If the PCI seems more democratized, more liberalized and freer of Soviet influence, in reality—and this is proven by the attacks that have been made upon it—its the French party that the Soviet Union fears the most. In substance what this means is that the communist party of a country more habituated to liberty is more frightening to the USSR than the strongest communist party in the Western world—that is, the PCI.

It was inevitable, I repeat, that the Right get a second wind in Europe, since the communist Left didn't know how to keep in step when it came to both national and international politics. Let's return to Portugal for a moment. In Paris I met a Portuguese housewife who summed up ten years of her country's history in one comment: "In the days of Salazar it was terrible, but there was dried cod. Now things are going better, but there's no dried cod anymore." Whether one likes it or not, a large part of humanity sees things in precisely these terms: it thinks of bread, of dried cod, or in the luckiest cases, of beefsteaks and automobiles. Let's be frank: if today in Italy the United States cut off its aid and vetoed the entrance of the communists into the government, what could the communists do (supposing, of course, that the political class was willing to ignore the American veto) except play the policeman and administer the nation's poverty? And if the PCI enters the government with the backing of the Americans, it will be everything but a communist party: it will become a duplicate of the Christian Democrats.

* * *

MARCELLE PADOVANI. And so, whatever the hypothesis, for you the conclusion has to be the same: the PCI, and more generally the Western communist parties as a whole, serve no purpose; formerly, they served as a not always effective opposition; today, they are of no further use at all.

LEONARDO SCIASCIA. In as much as I do not have the feeling that the day is near when the working classes will accede to the government of things—even if accession to the government represents a useful and edifying utopia, which helps to stir society—I think that the one service the PCI can render to Italy is to represent fully the classes that provide its strength, and to fulfil the function of a firm, rigorous, and above all competent opposition. Thus I continue to believe that Rivarol's truth is, alas, everybody's truth.

MARCELLE PADOVANI. It does sometimes happen, however, that these masses bring about revolution or, more commonly, succeed in achieving managerial control over ever more substantial "pieces" of society...

LEONARDO SCIASCIA. There will always be somebody who will manage affairs in their stead and in their name, and, like it or not, those managers of new realities will also be middle-class. The bourgeoisie is an undying category. The best we can do is to proceed in such a way that this bougeoisie be the best possible.

MARCELLE PADOVANI. Let's focus for a moment on the "Italian case." It is generally allowed that one of the PCI's merits is to have been, ever since the turning point at Salerno in 1944, something other than a sterile opposition, and, moreover, never to have confined itself to opposition, and to have demonstrated its sense of its "responsibilities" in accepting to "manage," nay, to promote a politics of austerity in such a way as to exercise maximum control over its effects on the workers' lives. What interest could these same workers have in seeing the PCI move into the opposition?

Leonardo Sciascia. For workers having a job, a PCI seeking the historic compromise may perhaps do. The problem, for the parties of the Left, is the unemployed, the South, the young people. To a PCI that is no longer in the opposition, that knows nothing of opposition, what now are the unemployed, the South, the young people? They are problems to set aside. Well, it is crazy to talk only about workers who are "busy"; there are other ones too, and they must be reckoned with.

Marcelle Padovani. Your view seems to be that all parties amount to the same thing, that power can only corrupt, that it is better to leave it in the hands of the middle class. Basically, isn't your message identical to that of the young New Philosophers in France?

Leonardo Sciascia. My attitude toward politics is comparable to Unamuno's toward the Christian religion. Unamuno didn't believe in the immortality of the soul, but he lived as though he did. I do not for my part consider that politics has anything grand about it; rather, I consider it a mediocre activity reserved for mediocre people. I do not believe that we will ever achieve anything perfect, just, and altogether free in the way of political and social organization, but that it is necessary to live and struggle as though we were convinced that we will.

I look upon power not as something demoniacal, but as something blunt and inimical to the true liberty of man. Be that as it may, my inclination is to struggle in order that, within the power structure, changes be possible, that there be the possibility of alternatives, of innovations, of a better organization of justice, an ever greater amount of freedom, and so I involve myself as soon as there is a battle to fight. I am very well aware that I have in me a certain spirit of contradiction, but I also know that it must inhabit every man engaged in an intellectual activity. Borges said: "I enrolled in the conservative party, but never did the victory of the radicals give me so much pleasure as then." Such, I think, must be the position of an intellectual. If he wishes to succeed in understanding the things he's fighting against ...

MARCELLE PADOVANI. If, as has happened in the past, there were a revolt against the state in Sicily, would you agree to support it?

LEONARDO SCIASCIA. I would more willingly support a revolt in favor of the state. For in Sicily the state has never existed, it materialized only once, and that was under fascism (which is why I sometimes take alarm when I hear talk about the state): fascism then presented the image of a serious state, which managed to win respect even from the church and didn't hesitate to take on the Mafia. I have no nostalgia for that state.

In return I would like indeed to found, or see founded, a democratic state capable of putting the Constitution into practice. Then, yes, I would be able to support such a movement: if it were loyalist and constitutional. For though the Italian Constitution may have some defects, it still represents the best charter of liberties that the Italian people have had up to now.

MARCELLE PADOVANI. If all the parties, including the PCI, are so disappointing, then what can a citizen who wishes to change society or, more simply, to live a better everyday existence, do? Your character Candido flees in the direction of Paris; does his departure symbolize the fact that there is nothing more to hope for in Italy?

LEONARDO SCIASCIA. There is always something to hope for. Men are not done with their thinking, there will be other ideas, other utopias, other cosmogonies will be born. They may not always point in the right direction, obviously. For example, I believe that at the present time every serious person can only be disturbed to observe the conditions emerge for the outbreak of a Third World War: if we were to feed all the data on the world situation into a computer, its response would be: inevitable war. On the other hand, this does not mean that men should not struggle to avoid it. I believe also that in the future there will be political parties capable of renewing themselves, of adapting to reality—the most sclerosed at the moment being the PCI.

MARCELLE PADOCANI. Sometimes one seems to make out a kind of hatred for Italy in your remarks.

LEONARDO SCIASCIA. I hate and detest Sicily in so far as I love it, and in so far as it does not respond to the kind of love I would like to have for it. I can extend this sentiment to the whole of Italy. I was born here, I am therefore condemned to love this country, yet at times I'm seized by a wild desire at least not to die here... It would in some way compensate for the fact of having been born here. That sentence of Lawrence's that I have already quoted—"There was no doubt not a single cultivated person in Sicily, otherwise he would have fled the place long ago"—is probably an erroneous statement with no correspondence to reality, yet it is correct that in Sicily the intellectuals still constitute a foreign body. They exist, but they are unable to live in this society, and that's what it comes to: it's as if the entire social fabric were bent on rejecting them. I am obliged to acknowledge this as regards myself: I behold this sort of existential whirlwind—so alive, so fascinating—which wakens in about everybody that Stendhalian benevolence with which it has become habitual to look at Italy. But there's none of that order, none of that clarity in relations among classes, categories, and individuals, which would be indispensable in a democratic society. For centuries the intellectual has been considered something marginal, esthetic, decorative. The poet's, the writer's principal function was to embellish life—the life, of course, of those classes which were in proper condition to enjoy life. At a certain point this intellectual shifted from the role of beautifier to that of the man who seeks to understand. And this intellectual was condemned to a kind of estrangement; he became a foreigner in his own land. When Moravia was reproved for his silence—as I was reproved for mine—about terrorism during the Moro affair, he replied by referring to his "painful estrangement," declaring that he identified with nothing the Red Brigades were doing, but did not identify either with anything the political class had been doing over the last thirty years. Here he posed the problem of the presence or, rather, the absence of the intellectual in our country. In effect, it's not he who does not see how he fits into the course of things, but the course of things that ignores him. It's a condition that one passively submits to. This country, well, it has no use for mirrors that reflect it, for sciences that focus upon it. Italy needs to live in an indefinite present, in an amorphous, shapeless, colorless, and unforeseeable today. The intellectual, who normally represents the presence of the past and concern for the the future, is for that very reason dismissed, rejected, exiled.

*   *   *

MARCELLE PADOVANI. But is not the intellectual also responsible for his own status and condition?

LEONARDO SCIASCIA. He might be responsible for them if he had truly had a function. But he has never had one, in Italy, from Machiavelli's time to our own. Machiavelli noted that "They don't even have us look under a stone," and he meant that "Those in power do not assign us anything to do." I think likewise of Alberto Moravia. Not so much of Moravia the novelist, who sometimes gives an impression of abstraction, of remoteness from life, but of the Moravia who is always present on the subject of things Italian, the Moravia who has something of the journalist, if I may put it that way, whose judgment is always precise and lucid. In what Moravia has said from the fascist period up until today, Italy has always refused to see any reflection of itself.

I myself am often assailed by doubts as to whether my books have served any purpose at all, so clear is the absence of critical consciousness in the unfolding of Italian reality. I wonder to myself: the three million copies of books of mine that must have been sold in this country, to whom have they been of use? What has been their impact? And I think again of that faraway novelist Manzoni and his *The Betrothed*, which presents such a pitiless picture of Italy: entire generations of Italians have read it, millions and millions of adults and adolescents. If we ask ourselves how it was read and what purpose it served, dissected as it was in all the schools of the peninsula, one is obliged to admit that it served no purpose, or almost none, that it passed like water under bridges. You get the impression, discussing it with one of the Italians who vaguely remembers having read it, that he didn't understand anything in it, and that he is talking, not about the book fraught with religious, moral, and civic disquiet, but rather about a book whose job is to absolve the Italians of their sins with regard to religion.

MARCELLE PADOVANI. Have you had the same impressions upon reading the reviews of your own books?

LEONARDO SCIASCIA. Reviews of my books have rarely interested me; I remember very little about them. I must say that the best one, the best not because it said nice things about me but because I found it the most useful, was written by Salvatore Battaglia, who had a philological background and knew how to read the heart of a text. The reviews from the communist side were the worst: they made their judgments according to whether I was drawing closer to or moving away from the party. It was amusing, actually. But every now and then, in connection with each of my books, there were sound reviews. I recall certain articles by Gramigna, Vigorelli, Cavallari... And then the French critics in general; I know that I owe the most discerning pages to Dominique Fernandez, Claude Ambroise, Philippe Renard.

On the whole, however, the balance isn't positive. In the past I kept a little tally, and here's what I found: seven out of ten reviewers hadn't read, or entirely read, the book that they were struggling to criticize; their resumé would be totally erroneous. There's even a book by a woman called *Sciascia's Sicily* who makes no mention of the book I did on Sicily, *La corda pazza*, and who, in addition, has the hero of *A Man's Blessing* run over by an automobile, an ending that I and its readers were unaware of.

MARCELLE PADOVANI. After this incursion into the function of the intellectual, I am going to ask that we return to politics, and to that kind of dissecting of power that you have performed in your work. We have talked about the Mafia, about the communist party, but not yet about that Italian "specialty," the Christian Democrats. It is generally not understood abroad how the DC, like the Eastern European communist parties, could have become a "party-state."

LEONARDO SCIASCIA. I think that in order to discuss the DC you need to "take a step backward"—as they say in novels—and return to the days of fascism. At the end of the fascist period, they used to tell the joke about how "Italy has ninety million inhabitants: forty-five million fascists and forty-five million antifascists." It is certain, in any case, that the consensus around fascism was just about absolute, at least from the signing of the Concordat until the the war in Abyssinia. Then after 1936 some criticism was addressed to the regime on the theme of principles and usages: Mussolini proclaiming himself Marshal of the Empire, Starace imposing certain rites, the numerous cases of illegal acquisition of wealth. But fascism didn't really fall out of favor with the Italians until the moment when it declared war, and above all when the United States declared war on it.

MARCELLE PADOVANI. Nevertheless, the history books tell of massive resistance to fascism in the form of a veritable "people's war" following Italy's entrance into the conflict, and, even before it, speak of many persons going underground resistance, of many voluntary exiles after the outlawing of the labor unions and democratic parties. Not to mention the reactions to the vexations inflicted on the regime's opponents, the castor oil forced down their throats . . .

LEONARDO SCIASCIA. The castor oil used to get a big laugh, they would refer to it as if to a goliardery, a students' prank. Well, you understand, fascism had put an end to strikes, got rid of political parties, restored public order, curbed the Mafia, and assured stability of the currency: public employees or professors who earned five hundred lire a month knew that on that five hundred lire they would be able to live decently during the month. To be sure, a minority of Italians deplored fascism and its exactions, but it was only a minority that benefitted from no general solidarity. As for me, I began to frequent antifascist milieux in 1938, at age seventeen; there they invoked Turati, the Rosselli brothers, and Count Sforza, but it wasn't until after the war was over that I heard the name of Antonio Gramsci pronounced for the first time.

Christian Democracy made its appearance in Italian political life after the war. It got its success from presenting itself right away as a reassuring party, capable of guaranteeing continuity—and not only juridical, but also historic, ideological, and human continuity—with fascism. Its leader, Alcide de Gasperi, had not spent time in jail for antifascism; the known antifascists among the Christian Democrats were so few in number that Italians had the correct impression that the DC's declarations of antifascism were purely formal. And here, too, we had better go back for a moment. The DC's ancestor, the Popular Party, which included a good number of militant Catholics before the war, had never been taken seriously in Italy. During my childhood, when someone spoke of it, it was always with contempt, and as preparation for telling a few jokes. Of a distant relative of mine who was a member of the Popular Party it used to be said, in order to emphasize his lack of virility, uselessness, and unintelligence, that it was no wonder if he had become that way, since he had been a *pipino*, that is, a member of the PP. And as for Don Sturzo, founder of the PP, he was dismissed as "that priest with the long nose who used to meddle in politics..."

I say all this to stress that, from the beginning, the Christian Democrats were something altogether different from the PP: they were taken seriously from the start precisely because they were the heirs of fascism. The network of priests took on the job of mobilizing the population in favor of the new party, just as they had done for the fascists: mystic crusades, miracles, weeping Madonnas, bleeding Christs, *vergini pellegrine*, propaganda centered around Father Lombardi, the announcer on Radio Vaticano also known as "God's microphone"—there was nothing they didn't resort to, especially at election time, with a view to creating a consensus around the DC. However, the simplest and most profound consent came straight from the fact that, despite the "democratic" on its label, the DC was nothing of the kind. And I must say that on this score it did not susequently disappoint: the Italian Constitution, which is one of the best in the world, remained, through the fault of the DC, unapplied for a long time by the DC, and it only began to be applied when, seeing itself weakened, the Christian Democrats agreed to govern with the socialists within a "center-left" framework. For so long as it was assured of running the political show, the DC did not undertake the slightest reform. Thus it was not until 1964 that the party allied itself with the socialists, even looking for a way to devour them. The business of seduction went well at first, thanks to the dividing up of cabinet and other posts in the higher and lower echelons of power. But it succeeded only in part, thanks to the great disorder that reigned within the core of the socialist party: there you found persons who could have figured in any party, antifascists, sincere democrats, lovers of liberty, and finally socialists. If the PSI had been more compact, if it had been untroubled by the slightest internal divisions, and animated by more homogeneous human and political types, the rapprochement with Christian Democracy and the sharing out of jobs would have completely destroyed it. Thus, while incontestably putting itself in hock to corruption, the PSI was able to obtain certain things in exchange, such as the Workers' Charter.

* * *

MARCELLE PADOVANI. How is it that a party so obviously corrupt as the Christian Democrats, a party so discredited, can continue to organize such impressive numbers of workers and peasants, that is to say, preserve the confidence of the very people who, in the final analysis, are those who pay the costs of the DC's political and economic choices?

LEONARDO SCIASCIA. The Christian Democrats have nothing of the state about them. Furthermore, they don't promise the moon and stars to anyone. Neither the rational organizing of the economy. Nor a good administration. Nor a just court system. And it's precisely because they are not the state and do not promise the state to the Italians that the Italians are so pleased by them. The idea of the state frightens my compatriots—a state which, above all if it is democratic, advocates or imposes certain choices, which obliges you to reflect, to ask yourself questions, to give thought to the consequences of this or that political decision. With a state of that sort the Italians don't want to have anything to do—and I am speaking, naturally, of the majority of the Italians who gravitate around Christian Democracy.

Also, the DC has demonstrated a particular capacity (for the DC this was hardly difficult) for utilizing the concept of Christian charity in order to create a capillary network of interests based on public assistance: pensioned invalids are very numerous in Italy, more numerous than in any other part of the world. Except that they are not really invalids. Such is Christian Democracy's power base, above all in Sicily and in the South. Morever, I believe that if we decided to pass in review all the legislative activity of the Sicilian Regional Assembly, it would emerge that the greatest percentage of decrees have to do with social welfare.

* * *

MARCELLE PADOVANI. Antonio Gramsci, the PCI theorist, said that in the end it was better that often illiterate, isolated, and ignored masses be organized under the banners of the Popular Party— which later became the DC—rather than remain all alone in their little corner, without possible access to even a glimmer of collective consciousness. According to Gramsci, these masses were bound little by little to discover, beyond welfare, their stake in democracy and socialism, abandoning the DC and chosing the camp of socialism.

LEONARDO SCIASCIA. The problem that presents itself to me is to determine whether these masses are or aren't truly organized by the DC. And if by chance they are organized, whether it's not simply a matter of a lot of iron filings clustered to a magnet. For my part I feel that the Christian Democrats' success resides in their being the precise opposite of what Gramsci thought: a disorganization pure and simple, or in any case a non-organization. Living exclusively, as I see it, on its capillary relationships with small clienteles, it is incapable of mobilizing the masses upon which it exerts influence; I see this best illustrated whenever we have a referendum. What do you imagine the Christian Democrat cadres do when there is an upcoming vote of this sort, which implies a direct relationship between the central authority and the citizens? They do nothing; they abstain from issuing directives, from participating in campaigns, from the least bit of propagandizing. And so it is that almost all the referendums in Italy have been won by the Left. Ask the DC to go over the heads of its intermediate cadres, it evaporates; it is able to realize itself fully only when there are elections, when the political connection is established through persons and not through ideas. Then the current flows. Christian Democracy is a party without ideological justification.

* * *

MARCELLE PADOVANI. From Christian Democracy as a power we might perhaps now move on to the church as an institution and to Catholics as a body of believers. "I have never encountered a Catholic, and I'm almost ninety-two years old," says one character in *A Man's Blessing*. Somewhere else one of your characters maintains that "Italian Catholics don't exist," that they are "an invention of Gramsci." And to your doubts about the authenticity of Italian Catholics' faith you sometimes even add a frankly anticlerical, anti-religious temper: it's on the road to Lourdes that your Candido loses his virtue, and ends up being the only one among all the pilgrims to be miraculously healed. In *Antimony* one reads: "From having done nothing for ten years, I have convinced myself that when they talk about death, what they are referring to is God, that every man carries within himself the God of his own death." And in your letter to the archbishop of Palermo you finally evoke those Catholics who brandish their faith like a crucifix, using it to beat about the head and shoulders whatever worthy people they find standing on street corners. Don't these continual provocations have an essentially pedagogic value? Aren't there distinctions to be made between the reality of faith in Northern Italy and its more or less superficial character in the South? Isn't there a contradiction between the content of your books and the things you said early on in this interview about being a "religious man"?

LEONARDO SCIASCIA. My books contain a certain number of generalizations behind which there is a plainly provocative intention. Today I could perhaps say that, yes, I am able to detect a few Catholics, and even that, in my opinion, a great return to Catholicism is in the offing, but a Catholicism taught in a different way, a not very "Italian" way in comparison to the past. This searching for religion as a refuge comes, I believe, from the religious disillusionment brought on by Marxism.

The overall situation in Italy from the point of view of religion? An almost total absence of religious spirit, and a manner of living one's faith in an exclusively superstitious register. Scratch the average Italian and you find a basic anticlericalism. Personally, I don't believe I'm anticlerical; I describe the Italian and Sicilian clergy such as it is— ignorant, rapacious, and substantially atheistic. I very much wish that there were many good priests; some exist, but they are few. In the same way, how pleased I would be if these people lived more intensely the religion they officially profess.

You know, the Sicilian people, like any other people, find themselves standing before life as if before a mystery, to which the keys, in this case, are the church, the saints, the miracles, although none of these notions has much to do with the Gospel. While in the North of Italy the religion took hold more or less autonomously in respect to political life, here in the South the rival factions had each chosen a saint as its emblem: whence the celebrated "wars of the saints" that are still recalled in theatricals in Sicily. That is why the clergy's taking one political side or another has such a factious character there. Once again I shall speak about my own village where, even though it was never the scene of a "war of the saints," a pitched battle was fought with our neighbors from Castrofilippo. The Madonna di Fatima was the bone of contention. The Castrofilippo people had kept it for a certain period of time, and the moment had come when delegates from Racalmuto were to take delivery of the effigy at the church in Castrofilippo. But the Castrofilippesi weren't in agreement: they themselves wanted to carry the Madonna to Racalmuto themselves, after traversing the whole of our village. Thus it was that there took place the fiercest battle ever seen thereabouts, in the course of which the Madonna was showered with epithets and curses from both sides. Amongst us, religion has always been utilized for other things than the requirements of faith.

A few more words about the patron saints of cities and villages. For example, the cult of Santa Rosalia in Palermo: it derives its origin from the plague, which raged in the Sicilian capital at a time when it was under the high protection of Saint Christine. And it continued, and it decimated the population, the prayers and the gifts to that saint notwithstanding. Then the Palermitani, who are realists, decided to change patron saints, and turned to Santa Rosalia for help. The plague subsided, then ceased. Clearly, my compatriots treated Santa Cristina like some old Mafia chieftain whose power had waned and who was fated to be replaced by some younger, more dynamic *capomafia*. You see, in the mind of the Sicilian, celestial affairs unfold in just the way earthly ones do: up there too you have your *capomafia*, godfathers, informers, and Mafiosi.

Today however it can be said that something has changed: the men of the Sicilian church are not fundamentally different from those of the Italian church. Cardinal Ruffini, archbishop of Palermo, was probably the last strong personality called upon to run the affairs of the church in the old style. He did so authoritatively, intervening in every domain; claiming property which, according to certain documents in his possession, should have been returned to the church; building places of worship wherever he saw fit (he even had a chapel raised and dedicated to Sant' Ernesto—certainly the only one in all of Italy—because that was his saintly namesake); interfering in the selection of candidates for the Christian Democrat slates; never hesitating to put in his oar when it came time to appoint public officials or nominate university professors; and, finally, condemning anybody who, in his presence, spoke of Mafia, going so far as to deny its existence. A true Renaissance cardinal. A native of Mantua in the North of Italy, he had succeeded wonderfully in acquiring a Sicilian-Mafioso mentality.

MARCELLE PADOVANI. You have taken a deep interest in the Inquisition as an extreme the church permitted itself and as an institution which is an offense to human reason and to human rights. Why this interest, since in Sicily there weren't even any heresies to combat?

LEONARDO SCIASCIA. I interested myself in the Inquisition because the Inquisition's existence in the world is a long way from being over. There is a Polish writer who says: "Beware of telling your dreams, the psychoanalysts may end up in power." For my part I consider that it has come to that already: the sociologists and the psychoanalysts *are* in power! During the Moro affair we were able to witness them in high gear, called in as they were to analyze the messages and behavior of the Red Brigades, without, however, producing any very conclusive results. But we all know of countries where sociologists and psychiatrists have shown their ability to serve those in power. The Inquisition has shifted its abode to such people, and they have carried it on exactly as in times past. In my quarrel with Amendola I pointed out how "inquisitory" his language was, how reminiscent of the old Catholic Inquisition. I had the same feeling when they got after me over my silence during Moro's kidnapping: I was appalled, and am still appalled, by what appeared to be a case of an Inquisition even more terrible than the ancient one. For, after all, the olden times Inquisition put you on trial for the things you said, but not for silence. Even fascism itself was satisfied if you kept your mouth shut!

MARCELLE PADOVANI. Don't you think you were reprimanded for your silence during the Moro affair mostly because you had been in the habit of speaking up on Italy's foremost problems?

LEONARDO SCIASCIA. I was reproved for being silent—better, I was accused of being silent. Now, if I said nothing it was because at the time I had nothing to say. I was in the grip of confusion, I felt myself assailed by great pity, and I thought that I needed to square things with my conscience, not with my inquisitors.

MARCELLE PADOVANI. This led you to write *The Moro Affair* . . .

LEONARDO SCIASCIA. I wrote it not because I felt guilty about having said nothing, but because, at a certain point, I had something to say. My interest in Moro was propelled by my old idea that one must to seek the truth. His is a terrible story, not only because of its tragic end, but because it was drowned in a sea of rhetoric and mystification. It seems to me that people were bent on modifying those very things in the image of this man that made him most human. Perhaps Moro the prisoner of the Red Brigades was afraid. Perhaps his foremost thought was of survival. But he always behaved like the man he had been: why claim that he had become different? In short, I wanted to write more a religious book than a political book.

MARCELLE PADOVANI. Did you imagine yourself in Moro's place?

LEONARDO SCIASCIA. I imagined myself in his place as much as in the place of any prisoner. I understood his suffering and anguish, and I felt compassion for him, compassion in the original sense of the word. Throughout those terrible fifty-five days he was on my mind all the time, and the whole while I thought that an adventure of this kind could only happen to him. I'm convinced that he was more intelligent than his captors and that, in a certain sense, he got the better of them. He was human, they were only capable of being bureaucratic automatons. The only messages of love, of youth, and of life were the ones that came from him; from the others there came only the outdated, the worn-out, the *déjà vu*. The *brigatisti* are in my opinion veterans of the underground, some among them must have spent time in prison during the Resistance. There is a great ideological and human senility in the messages they planted. Who would dare contend that Moro was not worth more than those men?

MARCELLE PADOVANI. Your resignation from the Palermo city council, and then the Moro affair, appeared to have definitively distanced you from any commitment to party politics. However, in May 1979 you decided to join the Radical Party ticket, despite that party's lack of any program, its wild-card role in the scheme of Italian politics, and the heterogeneity of the votes it attracts (I am thinking particularly of the *montanelliani* votes). Don't you fear the political and ideological imbroglio of the Radical Party? What do you expect from your presence in the European Parliament?

LEONARDO SCIASCIA. Hemingway said, "I don't write books, it's books that write me." To parody him: it wasn't me who decided to become a Radical Party candidate, but the books I've written over the last few years. And especially the one that could be considered the least political of all, *The Mystery of Majorana*. As for ideologies, I'm no longer worried when a party lacks an ideology; what worries me are the parties that stir up ghosts, the phantoms of ideologies. And as for programs, can we honestly say that the parties which have claimed to have them over the past thirty years have even begun to create the conditions to carry them out? If we cast just a glance at the schools, the hospitals, the transportation system, the police, the administration of justice, the state industries, the libraries, the museums, and at every last thing having to do with the state, we're seized by dismay. And we can begin to free ourselves from such dismay only by becoming a trifle conservative, by going back over the chain until we reach the weak link. The only way to be revolutionary is to be something of a conservative. Unlike the reactionary, who wants to return to things at their worst, the conservative is someone who wants to start from the best, who wants to conserve the best. And we must admit that the schools, at least, were once a bit better.... The schools are the place to start all over again.

As for your last question about the European Parliament, all I can say at the moment is: I'm going to have to see. With great suspicion, with such skepticism. But we'll have to see.